Shining Through The Darkness

Sermons For The Winter Season

Michael D. Wuchter
submitted by Shirley Dyer Wuchter

Shirley Dyer Wuchter

CSS Publishing Company, Inc., Lima, Ohio

SHINING THROUGH THE DARKNESS

Most scripture quotations are from the New Revised Standard Version of the Bible, copyright 1989 by the Division of Christian Education of the National Council of the Churches
of Christ in the USA. Used by permission.

Scripture quotations marked (REB) are from the Revised English Bible copyright © Ox-
ford University Press and Cambridge University Press, 1989. Used by permission.

Scripture quotations marked (GNB) are from the Good News Bible, in Today's English
Version. Copyright © American Bible Society, 1966, 1971, 1976. Used by permission.

Scripture quotations marked (TLB) are taken from The Living Bible © 1971. Used by permission of Tyndale House Publishers, Inc., Wheaton, Illinois 60189. All rights reserved.

Scripture quotations marked (RSV) are taken from the Revised Standard Version of the
Bible, copyrighted 1946, 1952 ©, 1971, 1973, by the Division of Christian Education of
the National Council of the Churches of Christ in the USA. Used by permission.

Library of Congress Cataloging-in-Publication Data

Wuchter, Michael D.
    Shining through the darkness : sermons for the winter season / Michael D. Wuchter.
        p. cm.
    ISBN 0-7880-2482-5 (perfect bound : alk. paper)
    1. Lutheran Church—Sermons. 2. Church year sermons. 3., Sermons, American—20th
century. I. Title.

BX8066.W83S35 2006
252'.041—dc22

                                                                    2007032080

For more information about CSS Publishing Company resources, visit our website at
www.csspub.com or email us at csr@csspub.com or call (800) 241-4056.

Cover design by Barbara Spencer
ISBN-13: 978-0-7880-2482-5
ISBN-10: 0-7880-2482-5   PRINTED IN USA

*With love and a grateful heart for
all who provided and provide prayers
and their own light,
especially my family*

*Andrew Dyer Wuchter
and
Jennifer Kirsten Wuchter Brown*

*their spouses
Traci Elaine Gehring Wuchter
and
Robert Andrew Brown*

*and
my granddaughter
Eleanor Grace Brown*

"Waiting" and "traveling a journey" are themes that run through these sermons on biblical texts for Advent and Epiphany. Michael Wuchter brought pastoral concerns to preaching for a campus community at Wittenberg University, and the global interests of a university and the church to his words for congregations in New Jersey and Minnesota. His insights, stories, and reflections continue to inspire, as we wait and journey.

John Reumann
Emeritus Professor of New Testament
Lutheran Theological Seminary at Philadelphia

Michael Wuchter was a master of the English language and an excellent, excellent preacher.

Jerry L. Schmalenberger
Former President
Pacific Lutheran Theological Seminary

From recounting a visit to the grotto in Bethlehem or meeting Mother Teresa in India, to sharing conversations with his own children around the family table, Michael Wuchter's sermons weave the poetry of solid incarnational theology, artful storytelling, a passion for peacemaking, and the humble confessions of faith of a husband, father, teacher, and community leader. Wuchter's sermons share his heart for justice and concern for the marginalized, his love of family and friends, and his deep sense of responsibility to utilize his gifts and experience in service to the larger community within the church and society. His sermons provide sound exegetical content for the academic, pique the imagination of the parish pastor, and offer rich devotional meditations for anyone seeking to center their lives more firmly in the gospel of God's grace and hope in Jesus Christ.

Linda Muhly
Pastor, St. Johannes Lutheran Church
New Milton, West Virginia

In a second volume of sermons, Michael Wuchter once again weaves together the ancient texts of the Bible with modern insights. His careful historical research and winsome stories combine for a rich tapestry of gospel proclamation. These sermons stretching from Advent through Epiphany form a sort of mosaic for the beginning of the church year — each story, each illustration, each wonderful tangent serving as tiles for a larger, clearer view of the one who came among us as the Word made flesh.

John D. Morris
Pastor, Prince of Peace Lutheran Church
Dublin, Ohio

These warm, conversational, well-illustrated, and textually based sermons will be helpful to any preacher or reader. Pastor Wuchter's sensitivity both to the text and to the context of his preaching lend an immediacy and relevance to his sermons. The sermons are seasonally appropriate and have a spiritual vigor that communicates the gospel of Christ to twenty-first-century listeners.

Arden L. Krych
Former Senior Pastor,
St. Matthew Lutheran Church
Springfield, Pennsylvania

In this remarkable collection of sermons, Michael Wuchter fully acknowledges a world rampant with violence and injustice that millions experience today. Against this backdrop of pain, he weaves with poetic creativity and sensitivity the acts of waiting, grieving, and hoping within and among personal, familial, and communal relationships. Long, cold winters are made shorter and warmer with these Christ-centered sermons in hand.

Daniel F. Martensen
Ecumenical Research Fellow,
Washington (DC) Theological Consortium
Former Director,
Dept. of Ecumenical Affairs, ELCA

There is always the necessary reminder of the resurrection in all of Michael Wuchter's sermons — even those accenting the incarnation themes of Advent, Christmas, and Epiphany. Wuchter's broad experience as a university and parish pastor shows clearly in his gospel proclamation as revealed in these timely messages.

Edwin Ehlers
Retired Bishop
New Jersey Synod,
Evangelical Lutheran Church in America

Wuchter displays his broad knowledge of biblical scholarship and interpretation in wide-ranging sermons for the winter season. Again and again he speaks of the ways in which God touches human lives. Drawing upon eclectic sources, both scholarly and personal, Wuchter challenges the reader to explore the meaning of this nexus in real-world, everyday living — at home, on the job, and with neighbors near and far.

Richard P. Veler
General Secretary of the University and
Professor of English Emeritus
Wittenberg University

Michael Wuchter's insights speak clearly because of their simplicity and their common sensibility. I appreciate his ability to cut through the clutter of our individual lives and show how Christ touches us in the midst of all that clutter — the "busyness" of our everyday business. Wuchter reminds us that the Christian experience is not just a middle-class American one, but is enriched and made more real by an understanding of the world around us, rich and poor, and of the international relevance and scope of Christ's message.

Thomas J. Evans
Assistant Director, Wisconsin Geological and
Natural History Survey
University of Wisconsin

Michael Wuchter has a gift for connections. His sermons connect the theological concepts of the winter with homey, familiar things in our lives. The waiting and longing of Advent connect with working a jigsaw puzzle; the joy of the Word made flesh connects with explaining the meaning of Christmas in 500 words or less to third-graders; the light of Epiphany cutting through the darkness connects with a hike in the woods at twilight. Yet we also find our lives connected with Mother Teresa of Calcutta, with neighbors in modern-day Nashville and Bethlehem, and with Greek divers and Martin Luther King Jr. How good it is to be reminded, especially in a season when isolation often happens, that God's grace connects us with God and our neighbors.

Carol Hertler
ELCA Pastor
Chillicothe, Ohio

Acknowledgments

No one will ever know if the sermons in this book would have been published in such a collection had my husband, The Reverend Doctor Michael David Wuchter not died so suddenly and prematurely. Because an initial collection of sermons, *Uplifting Christ Through Autumn: Sermons For The Fall Season*, evolved as a result of "Pastor Michael's" death, I would like to acknowledge the groups of people who helped me out of the dark tunnel of grief so that I could function to bring the first book and now the second book to fruition.

I think if Michael were alive, he would want his faith-filled and supportive parents, Robert and Eleanor Wuchter, as well as their entire family, acknowledged and thanked, and I join him.

I have two grown children who form my loving family: Andrew Dyer Wuchter and Jennifer Kirsten Wuchter Brown, and their spouses Traci Elaine Gehring Wuchter and Robert Andrew Brown, and now a granddaughter, Eleanor Grace Brown.

Locally, there was a group of people who made up my husband's prayer team and stayed together to pray with me weekly for a year. Thanks to Julie, Dave, Elaine, Don, and Glenn. That steady support and continuing ritual of prayer anchored me with my Creator and Comforter in a profound way.

Another group nurturing me out of deep grief to wholeness was formed, calling themselves the "velcro ladies." They promised to "stick with me," and these women — Kay, the two Beths, Normajean, and Gudrun, hovered over me like angels. Another friend and writer, Ann, came weekly and helped me persevere in the dream of publication.

Dave Benson, from the prayer group, let me know early on that he shared the vision of publishing Michael's writings. He offered to stand by me in the process, no matter what it took. We would meet periodically to set goals and eventually, he helped with editing.

My monthly Memoir Group, consisting of Martha, Kay, Jeanice, Destri, Margaret, Dorothy, and Donna, faithfully met for five years, prodding me in my writing and editing endeavors as did others in the Lake Superior Writers' Association.

Another set of friends, actually colleagues of my husband's when Michael was Pastor to the University at Wittenberg University in Springfield, Ohio, from 1979-1997, met with me yearly. Thanks to William Kinnison, President Emeritus; Dr. E. Charles Chatfield Jr., Professor of History; and Dr. Richard P. Veler, Professor of English and University Editor, for connecting me with CSS Publishing Company. Also, thanks to another significant colleague at Wittenberg, Sarah Tyree, my husband's personal secretary for eighteen years. Had it not been for these loyal companions and CSS Editor, Becky Allen, plus the reviewers, this collection would not have come to fruition.

Probably the people who fed my personal prayer life the most over time were the members of my Wednesday morning prayer group, often composed of different people at different times, yet all steadfast in their spiritual devotion. I am indebted to all of them.

So many people in congregations where Michael served and acquaintances of our family all across the nation and in a variety of places in the world encouraged me and, through prayer, sustained me. I believe this is an example of the power of prayer. I attribute God's Spirit at work in bringing about the first and now the second collection of sermons. I like to think God wants Michael's ministry to continue, now in a new form.

> — Shirley Dyer Wuchter
> wife of the late
> Reverend Doctor Michael D. Wuchter

Table Of Contents

Introduction

Simply put, Advent is a time of waiting, and Christmas marks the birth of Christ, who was Emmanuel — God with us — God's love sent in the form of a human being like us. Epiphany is the in-breaking of God's presence into our lives, the light of Christ breaking through the darkness of the human condition.

I find that the concept of waiting and traveling a journey through Advent to the long awaited Christ-event and experiencing the epiphany of Christ has taken on new meaning for me. I have gone through a waiting period of sorts, what most people would call grief, when my husband of almost 31 years of marriage died suddenly of heart failure in Namibia, Africa, while we were on a mission trip. My whole world changed in a few minutes. Since that point in time, for the past six years, I have been waiting to see if I would ever become "normal" again; I even asked myself, what is normal? But like Advent leading to Christmas and Epiphany following Christmas, my journey progressed to a fulfillment. The light returned after the darkness. My days of insecurity, uncertainty, wandering, and wondering, waned. Asking what meaning and mission God had for my life became less desperate and eventually was revealed in part. Life as I had known it was now not only changed but also made new. Much like the people of old anticipated Christ's coming, then rejoiced in the new birth, I, too, traveled my personal journey, then celebrated in becoming my transformed self. Christ's love broke into my life and lifted the darkness.

My prayer is that these sermons from the winter season of the church year will take you on a journey that is as surprisingly rich and as amazingly fulfilling as it was for me as I read and reread these sermons on my healing journey to wholeness.

— Shirley Dyer Wuchter
January 7, 2006
Duluth, Minnesota

Advent Vespers
Isaiah 9:5-7; 1 John 1:1-4; Luke 1:26-31; John 1:14a

Incarnation In Nashville

The angel Gabriel was sent by God to a town in Galilee called Nazareth, to Mary. And Gabriel said to her, "Greetings, favored one! Do not be afraid! The Lord is with you. You will conceive and bear a son, and you will name him Jesus."   — Luke 1:26-31 cf

And the Word became flesh and dwelt among us.
     — John 1:14a (RSV)

She was shelling peas, apron-covered knees spread wide
     to catch each pea / each pod
I, shaky, needy / wandered near
Her ancient swollen hands / pushed back the hair / that
     hid my face
She set down the pan / and, patting her knee,/ said:
oh, child / come on up here / and let me have a look at
     you /
Her voice was safe and so was I / sitting in the lap of
     God.[1]

Incarnation is a story about the physical, about us, about something one can see, touch, smell, and hold. It is a matter of substance, a matter of flesh and bone and mind, a matter of personhood. "... and the Word became flesh and dwelt among us ..." (John 1:14a RSV) "... and his name shall be called Emmanuel (which means, God with us)" (Matthew 1:23b RSV).

Incarnation — it is all in the story — for Mary did conceive and there was a birth as ordinary and miraculous as any birth, the newborn wrapped for warmth and security and placed to sleep in the fresh straw of a manger. The events that followed were as earthy, physical, and ordinary as our lives: water was poured over a traveler's body; a dance was performed to wedding music; the flesh of fish, firmed by heat and smoke, was separated and shared on a cold hillside; the hand of one critically ill was held securely. There were times when tears flowed, and there was the smell of death — the death of one who had been a beloved friend, dead, all wrapped and prepared for the grave. Large stones were hastily gathered to be used as killing weapons that were later dropped in the dust. Fresh, crisp bread was broken and eaten, the dinner wine-cup passed around for all to share. Thorns were forced into flesh in deliberate torture, a spearhead entering the body just under the rib cage. The Word took on this kind of flesh and the tangible things of our daily living and dying, all granting divine love *an entrance.*

"We declare to you what was from the beginning, what we have heard, what we have seen with our eyes, ... and touched with our hands, concerning the word of life — this life was revealed and we have seen it and testify to it" (1 John 1:1-2a).

Journalist Sue Halpern wrote an article titled "Values Which Are Simply There" in the *New York Times* magazine in 1990. The story is of a mother whose 32-year-old son lies dying of AIDS in a hospice. The mother comes every day, bringing a new dish that she has carefully prepared with love for her son. The son cannot swallow. Each day the food is stacked inside the small refrigerator next to the dishes from the previous days. The mother concedes that although her son could not swallow the food, he could at least smell what she has brought to him.

The mother speaks to the journalist of the strength within herself. She tells of her struggles, having come to our country from Guatemala and having to perform menial labor. Her English is limited and broken, but as she points to her heart, she says, "I am strong here. God is good. He gives me everything I ask for." She goes on to explain that people here expect instant results — quick answers — but God does not work that way.

The mother goes on to explain that her faith is also deep within herself — in her words, "deep in the ground." In the same way, she says she loves her son.

She asks the journalist to pray for her son. Ms. Halpern says that her prayer is for the son, but also for the devoted mother. Her prayer is that the young man dies soon.

During the interview and study, Ms. Halpern notices a book at the home where she is staying ... *Living In Truth* ... a book she has avoided looking at the whole time she has been there. She expresses the thought that there is nothing anyone can say about living or truth that would not be an abstraction — especially in the face of hospice care.

She began reading the first chapter and then she reread it and it prompted her to write the following:

> *In this world, categories like justice, honor, treason, friendship, infidelity, courage or empathy have a wholly tangible content, relating to actual persons and important for actual life. At the basis of this world are values which are simply there ... before we ever speak of them, before we reflect upon them and inquire about them. It owes its internal coherence to something like a pre-speculative assumption that the world functions and is generally possible at all only because there is something beyond its horizon, something beyond or above it that might escape our understanding and our grasp but ... firmly grounds this world, bestows upon it its order and measure, and is the hidden source of all the commandments, prohibitions and norms that hold within it.*[2]

When Ms. Halpern returns to the hospice the next day, she finds the distraught mother is not there. She has gone home, perhaps to prepare yet another untouched meal for her son who continues to lie the unmoving. Yet, even in his inert state, he gives back to his mother the love that she needs.

The tangible of our interwoven lives — giving divine love openings.

Isaiah wrote, "For all the boots of the tramping warriors and all the garments rolled in blood shall be burned as fuel for the fire ... For a child has been born for us ... named Mighty God; Everlasting; Prince of Peace ..." (Isaiah 9:5-6 cf).

He was born right here, in the real, the tangible of our living and dying, all now open for divine love. Incarnation is very real and present in substance and animation. Emmanuel — God with us. God in, with, and under the material reality of flesh and blood, mind and word, time and space, birth and death — offering a union that is tied to the final union. "The Christ" is what they called this centering point. "And the Word became flesh." Incarnation was God's self-disclosure.

In the words of theologian Carl Braaten, "Because of the real humanity of God in Christ, the wall of separation between the holy and the common, between the religious and the secular, between the soul and the body, between the world now and the one to come, between history and eschatology, between the natural and the supernatural — the perceived barrier separating each of these pairs has been shattered."

A few weeks ago, seventeen students and I went on a weekend service retreat. We went to Nashville, Tennessee. It could have been to just about any city in this country. Our retreat was basically an encounter with sisters and brothers who are on the margin — on the edge of physical health, on the edge of mental stability, and on the edge of apparent viability. The very small congregation that hosted us with great pride and exuberance was composed of basically three different types of people though now nicely, incredibly interwoven into the fabric of one family.

About a third of the congregation were women from the mission shelter down the street. Basically poor women, black and white, some holding babies or constantly reaching after scrambling toddlers. Many of these shelter women were physically and/or mentally ill; some I talked with said they often heard the voices of angels — perhaps Gabriel, most had tragic stories to tell of a family life that was laced with beatings and mental abuse and abandonment and chemical addiction. Some showed their scars more obviously than others.

Another third of the congregation were elderly women, who moved in the stiff, fragile way of the very old. They were the remnant of the factory workers of German ancestry that used to live in

18

the neighborhood before the factories closed and most of the factory families moved on. These women were, they once thought, marooned, abandoned with only memories and a sturdy little church building, a few old women.

The final third of the present congregation were younger persons but younger people with AIDS or those who knew the pain of recently losing close friends to AIDS.

And the setting for the sturdy little church: there is the women's shelter and abandoned factories and a government subsidized public housing project with a very active crack house three doors down the street from the church — a crack house with a tricycle on the front porch.

A member of the church was describing to me the mission of the congregation, of these ladies from the shelter, these old German women with Southern accents, these men with AIDS, and he paused and looked at me and said, "You know, for the most part, this congregation is composed of people who are all dying."

"A child has been born for us all named Mighty God; Everlasting Father; Prince of Peace — peace to be established and upheld with justice and with righteousness — right-ness — now and forevermore ..." (Isaiah 9:6-7 cf) reads the scriptural text for this evening.

Well, we joked and laughed and cried with and listened closely to those who were dying from AIDS; we listened to their stories and to their hopes for the future, all based on servanthood, on helping others who had lost hope; and we served a meal and then ate with the women and children from the shelter who also told us stories about blessings they have had in their life — like the care and love they receive in this little Nashville church. And the pastor talked to me about the neighborhood strategy against crack — a plan of action because "We care about the well-being of all our neighbors. We want to be the body of Christ right here!"

At our final meal in Nashville, we ate as much of the food as we possibly could that was lovingly offered to us by all the old German ladies who felt that we visiting Yankees were too skinny and if we were going to serve God at Wittenberg, we better eat a lot more of what they prepared for us and the members of this church:

turkey and dressing and potatoes and noodles and dumplings and four different kinds of pie — "try one of each!" We worshiped together and communed with them all — "body" and "blood." And in the congregation of the dying, there was a lot of life being offered, and it was very real and right and tangible, and it had flesh and future.

This evening's scripture reading is spoken again with contemporary urgency: "We declare to you what was from the beginning, what we have heard, what we have seen with our eyes, what we have looked at and touched with our hands, concerning the word of life — this life was revealed, and we have seen it and testify to it" (1 John 1:1-2a).

Incarnation is God's self-disclosure. Therefore everyday things can carry divine love: Maria's black bean soup and four kinds of Nashville pie, an old woman who pauses in the midst of shelling peas, you and me, and certainly bread and wine intermingled with the word. Creation and redemption can inter-penetrate each other; and human life is not external to the earth but part of the web of the natural, which one should not pollute or waste.

Incarnation validates the unity of spirit and flesh and future, and it calls us to be Christlike: to feed the hungry, clothe the naked, comfort the sorrowing, generate justice, and to know the peace and accept the grace, in all the tangible interactions that form our life together. "For a child has been born for us all."

"So we declare to you what was from the beginning, what we have heard, what we have seen with our eyes, ... and touched with our hands, concerning the word of life — there has been a glimpse of the final unity; we have seen it, and touched it and testify to it ..." (1 John 1:1-2a cf).

Sermon delivered November 14, 1990
Weaver Chapel
Wittenberg University
Springfield, Ohio

1. Martha Papson, "The Lap Of God," *Daughters of Sarah*, November/December 1987.

2. Sue Halpern, "Values Which Are Simply There," *New York Times* magazine, Hers column, 5/20/90 (Vol. 139, Issue 4824). It would be worth your time to look up this article and read it in its entirely, as it was given in the original sermon.

Behind The Brocade

> *In those days a decree went out from Emperor Augustus*
> *that all the world should be registered. This was the*
> *first registration and was taken while Quirinius was*
> *governor of Syria.* — Luke 2:1-2

From its beginning, the story of Jesus is anchored in specific human time and place, a time and place of human authority and arrogance, human power and manipulation — a time and place that we can all easily identify with today. This is the context for the coming of the Messiah.

From the very beginning of Luke's nativity story, the epitome of human power, the emperor gives an order that impacts the lives of everyone under his control, and there is no humility in the emperor's decree, "All the known world is to be registered." The emperor has spoken. Everyone is to go back to the male head-of-household's region of ancestral origin. According to tradition, this forced many families to endure a long journey often through dangerous territory.

"A decree went out from Caesar Augustus...." When I read this section of the text as I prepared for this sermon, I envisioned that torrent of refugees moving from Zaire back to Rwanda. It, too, is caused by political and military pressure. And most of the half a million Hutu on the move are peasant farmers and herders — poor families forced to move from one place to another. Interwoven in both stories is a sickening revelation of human greed and injustice, a struggle for power, deep distrust, centuries of cultural and tribal tension — even genocide. "In those days a decree went out from Emperor Augustus...." And so I have in my mind when I read this text from Luke, those television images of tens of thousands of

23

desperate refugees carrying bundles on their heads, frantic over lost children and the lack of food, all forced away from home — from Galilee to Judea, to the city of David called Bethlehem.

And in the crowd, Mary and Joseph did not stand out. We are not dealing here with the high priest's daughter or a regional, royal princess with valuable political ties, but rather a young peasant woman, who was engaged to a blue-collar laborer. She was forced to travel not to somewhere important — not to Jerusalem or Rome — not to a religious or political center, but rather to the outskirts of power — to little, dusty Bethlehem.

They stayed not in a regional palace or the guest house at a sacred shrine on some holy mountain but in a storage shed and animal stall. These are the kind of details within human history that are most often willingly forgotten out of embarrassment. The birth of the child was witnessed only by the mother and the father, although soon some ragtag shepherds still smelling of the fields arrived. We are talking here of lowliness, of ordinary poverty, of natural humility, and according to our faith tradition, incarnation! — God present even there — God tangible — coming even here.

While they were in Bethlehem, the time came for her to deliver her child. And she gave birth to her firstborn son and wrapped him in bands of cloth, and laid him in a manger, because there was no place for them in the inn. — Luke 2:6-7 cf

Later, Christians in western Europe envisioned the manger-crib in a wooden, free-standing barn filled with hay and heavy breathing cattle, like something one would find among poor German or English subsistence farmers. And this is okay — it captures in the symbol the lack of high status surrounding the coming of the Messiah. But in the Orthodox Christian tradition, stemming back to at least the third century AD, the stable was envisioned as a small cave in the low cliffs in the backyard — a common sight in Palestine today. This was a small, natural cave or rock overhang enlarged by the farmer, or innkeeper, to serve as a stable and storeroom. And in the little town of Bethlehem today there is a cave-like grotto that would have been in use around the time of Jesus. It could have served as an emergency birthing place for the poorest of the poor, for refugees on the move or other desperate visitors passing through the small village that had stood on that site for centuries upon centuries. Perhaps it was the birthing place of Jesus. It would certainly have been some place similar hidden in the mist of our ordinary living.

This small cave room is now located beneath the altar and the chancel floor of the medieval Basilica of the Nativity in Bethlehem. When I first visited the site a number of years ago, Orthodox and Armenian priests were bickering loudly about something — perhaps about the accidental use of the other's candles, or the allotted times for their separate worship services in the main nave of the basilica. Their argument removed for me any atmosphere of worship in the dark nave of that church. It seemed more like a noisy disagreement in a tavern or a crowded inn, some place that would have had little time for a poor couple seeking a place to rest.

Outside on Manger Square, in the center of the drab, little town of Bethlehem, there were strung gaudy Christmas lights of bright red and green and white — large bare bulbs swinging in the dry dusty wind, the black electrical cords strung from pole to pole like clotheslines. It was, as it is again this year, a tense time of distrust in Bethlehem. Israeli soldiers stood in clusters around the quiet square, peering around nervously, smoking cigarettes, holding compact submachine guns of black steel, searching with wide eyes the tops of buildings for trouble: for snipers or potential bombers. Small groups of Arab children on the square stared back. Some would bend down and pretend to pick up a stone to taunt the young soldiers. Just like this year, the fear of terrorism had kept many of the tourists away and the Arab wood-carvers who made their living selling small, olive wood manger scenes as souvenirs looked desperate. And there were shepherds out in the fields, keeping watch over their flocks by night, shepherd children in their early teens who should have been in school, but the Arab schools were all forced to close until the political tension abated. "And Joseph ... went from the town of Nazareth in Galilee to Judea, to the city of David called Bethlehem" (Luke 2:4).

25

What kind of setting is this for the coming of the Messiah? There is a parable that is circulating in Israel, Jordan, and Egypt. A scorpion in the Sinai desert asked a duck to carry him across the Red Sea to Egypt. The duck replied, "How foolish do you think I am? If I let you climb on my back, you will bite me and kill me with your poison."

"How foolish do you think I am?" the scorpion responded. "I can't swim; if I am on your back and bite you and you die, I will drown."

The argument, based upon reason and self-interest, convinced the duck, and he allowed the scorpion to climb onto his back. Halfway across the Red Sea the scorpion bit the duck.

"Why did you do that?" the duck demanded. "Now we will both die."

"You forget," said the scorpion, "this is the Middle East."

While they were there the time came for [Mary] to deliver her child.   — Luke 2:6

The pain we cause each other often doesn't make sense. This is the human world of injustice, of endured suffering, of sacrifice to get ahead of others, of revenge, and of inflicted pain.

In this day a decree went out from Emperor Augustus that all the world would be registered. But while they were there, in Bethlehem, it became time for Mary to give birth. And it seemed they were alone. They wrapped and laid the baby in an animal manger because there was no room for people like them in the hotels.

I went down the narrow steps behind the chancel of the Basilica of the Nativity, and I entered into the silent Christmas stable, though it seemed more like I was descending into a mausoleum. After my eyes adjusted to the low light of glass and gold chandeliers and the smoke from open oil lamps that smudged the stone ceiling into a mural of black thunderhead clouds, I saw gold brocade and ornate tapestries covering the walls, and the silver and gold framed icon paintings of dour saints. In one dark corner sat a sleepy, blinking priest, his hand out-stretched for donations. And there, near a metal star embedded in the stone floor, there before me was a plastic baby doll in a gold crib-like manger. This was the Christmas stable, in the little town of Bethlehem? This was it!

Why was I not disappointed? Why was I not disappointed in my pilgrimage to the manger?

If you parted the gold brocade and busy tapestries, if you pushed them aside, you could place your hand on solid rock. Isn't it precisely here in the Bethlehems of our co-existence, in the midst of human tensions, in the midst of persistent racism and threats of terror, in the midst of the flood of desperate refugees, in the center of misplaced values and gifts abused, in the times when religion seems to fall short of even its own desire for union and wholeness, when we want to enter something safe and reassuring and airy and we seem to find ourselves in something that is cave-like — that has the haunting feel of a tomb? Isn't it precisely here that God came — and still comes — on wings of forgiveness, a pliable love willing to be shaped into compassion, justice, and peace? Isn't it precisely here in the daily grotto of Bethlehem, where we live, with all its shortcomings and blessings, that we can, in faith, be guided to reach behind the gold brocade or worn tapestry and place our hands and souls on solid rock?

A child is born to us. Even here, wherever we are, there can be a God-empowered love — a God-based reality of forgiveness and guidance and hope beyond "the duck and the scorpion."

Incarnation is about touching God, and God touching us — and it is so physical. It is something we can see, and feel, and hold on to. God coming into our world is a matter of substance — of flesh and bone and mind, and compassion. It certainly can include us.

Incarnation spills out of the story of Jesus — from birth to death to life. For Mary did conceive, and there was a birth as ordinary and miraculous as any birth — a vulnerable newborn was wrapped for warmth and security and placed to sleep in the straw of a animal feeding trough. The events that followed the birth were also as real and earthy and physical and ordinary as our own lives. By the Jordan River, John poured water over a traveler's body, people danced to wedding music, the flesh of fish firmed by fire and smoke was separated and shared and eaten on a cold hillside, and the hand of one critically ill person was held securely. Fresh, crisp bread was broken, shared, and eaten together, the dinner wine cup passed around for all to drink — Jesus living in our world — but a world that also contained Caesar Augustus and still contains the emperor within each of us. This, too, is interwoven into the story — the rejection at the Bethlehem Inn — the slaughter of the innocents, when large stones were hastily picked up as weapons to kill a woman though dropped in the dust before Jesus and his pure acceptance of her. Jesus really touched and talked and ate with and healed and made whole, real people.

"In those days a decree went out from Emperor Augustus that all the world be registered." Thorns were forced into flesh in deliberate torture, a human being was nailed to a crossbar, and a spearhead entered the body just under the rib cage. God took on this kind of flesh, too. All the tangible things of our daily living and dying, all grant divine love an entrance to us, and desiring to flow through us to others — a love that holds the eternity of Easter.

> *The people who walked in darkness have seen a great light ... those who lived in a land of deep darkness — on them light has shined. For a child has been born for us, a son given to us ... [the] Prince of Peace....*
> — Isaiah 9:2, 6

> *We declare to you what was from the beginning, what we have heard, what we have seen with our eyes ... and touched with our hands, concerning the word of life — eternal life revealed: we have seen it, touched it, and testify to it.*　　　　— 1 John 1:1-2 cf

God in, with, and under the material reality of flesh and blood, mind and word, time and space, birth and death and life — incarnation is God's self-disclosure. Even in Bethlehem, lift up the brocade, the excess of our selfishness; push aside the worn tapestry — the superficial games we play to increase our status; push them aside wherever you may be now and touch the solid rock — the reality of God present — offered anywhere you are.

"While they were there, the time came for her to deliver her child." Come, Lord Jesus into our world and daily life, into our heart and soul, our mind and word. Use us to heal others in this hurting Bethlehem world of ours — this self-destructive realm of Emperor Augustus. Come, Lord Jesus, come.

Sermon delivered December 6, 1996
Weaver Chapel
Wittenberg University
Springfield, Ohio

Advent 1
Mark 13:24-37; Isaiah 64:1-9

Last Piece Of The Puzzle

Advent is the time of waiting, of wishing, and of wanting an intervention. Advent is a whisper, or a cry, or a prayer of "Come, Lord Jesus!"

As our member and artist, Teri, stated visually and verbally on our bulletin cover this morning, "Oh, that you would burst forth from the skies and come down ..." (Isaiah 64:1 TLB) or as the New Revised Standard Version translated the Hebrew of Isaiah 64, "O that you would tear open the heavens and come...." Come to us. "Please come, Lord Jesus!"

Advent is the season of "waiting," waiting for completion, waiting for things to be right — to be God intended.

One of our dear members died recently. She was a delightful, engaging woman. One certain thing about her was that right up to the time of her death, she was madly in love with her husband, but her husband died over 25 years ago. She told me that this separation was not right, not the way it was supposed to be. They were created for mutual support. In her great faith, she said that she was patiently waiting for reunion, that this was part of the promise of God. She was waiting for all creation to be complete, including herself. "Come, Lord Jesus!"

I find myself waiting much more than in years past. Our children have recently moved out of our home. It is not the same as when they were both away at college. Then our home was still, at least symbolically, their primary home. But our daughter is married now and living in lower Michigan. She and her husband work long hours and they care for a large herd of horses that demand daily attention. They live closer to my son-in-law's family, so when they do get away for a day or so, like at Thanksgiving, it is to be with others who are important to them. Our daughter cannot get to Duluth to visit very often. Our son, Andrew, moved to Minneapolis two weeks ago to begin a career search. I find myself waiting for them all to come home. I *long* for them to come home. But it is more than that. I long for other family reunions. I wish to be together to share a meal and conversation with my grandparents, but they are all now dead.

I find myself waiting for future children that I will love. I find myself waiting for the repetition of past moments when the power of loving union was so absorbing and so astonishing.

I long for the environment to be cleansed, for the air and water to be pure again, for mature white pines, for the cycle of life to be in harmony and beyond human selfishness.

I find myself waiting for things that I don't fully understand, for encounters and reunions and loving experiences that are beyond my comprehension. I wait for all of this, it seems. I long for this peace.

I think that this kind of longing, this waiting, is an innate part of all human beings. Various kinds of idols can momentarily redirect our wishes. If we are turned in upon ourselves, and our longing is only for our own enhancement at the expense of others, this denies our true self — the image of God within — God who creates in us a desire for the unity of all. But even when we let our sainthood dominate our life, we are waiting.

And as I get older, the waiting seems to have more power over my moods and thoughts and dreams. I think when we are young, if we are fortunate enough to be raised in a caring, creative, supportive setting, our waiting is dominated by the desire for personal fulfillment. When we are young, it seems that all of life is open for grand surprises, but also with the expectation that there are clear answers for all of life's multiple puzzles. But the older I become, it seems that waiting for a loving resolution to all things becomes more intense and urgent. "Come, Lord Jesus."

My wife, Shirley, is a guest teacher in some of our elementary schools in Duluth. She teaches a special curriculum about self-esteem and conflict resolution. A first-grade teacher told her about a lesson plan that she had intended to use in her class last week. It was to be a Thanksgiving bulletin board, titled "Things We Wish For." In the middle of the bulletin board was to be a large paper wishbone, like from a huge Thanksgiving turkey. Each child in the class was asked separately to name something that they wished for. The wishes were to be printed on various colored paper cards and then arranged in a festive manner around the wishbone on the bulletin board.

After collecting all the wishes, the teacher decided not to display them. The exercise was no longer celebrative. It revealed too much about these sacred children. The wishes were, for the most part, stories about incompleteness. These six-year-old children wished that their father would come home, that their older brother would stop hurting them, that their mother would stop drinking, and that their parents would get back together again. It seemed as if the whole class was waiting for some kind of loving completion.

Tear open the sky and come to us, dear God! Come and reveal your power. Shake the mountains, this earthly life's core; shake us and center us. We feel like leaves that whither and are blown away by the wind....
— Isaiah 64:1-6 cf

These tortured words of longing are from the book of Isaiah and formed our first scripture reading this morning. In its historical context, even though these Israelites who had been in forced exile in Babylon, were now allowed to return to the holy city of Jerusalem, something was still very wrong and incomplete. It seemed as though the focus of their culture now was on reestablishing power and status and favorable trade agreements, and the reappropriation of land. According to the prophet, even in the so-called "Holy City" there was an emptiness that lingered, a bitter taste, and among many, a nihilistic, malignant acceptance of incompleteness.

There was a sense of being swept toward an abyss, toward delusion, toward a final ending separated from the source and the purpose of justice and compassion, life groping in the darkness. They were experiencing a loss, a fear, a perception of one's very center decaying, or on the verge of flying apart. We are like clay. Do more than just form us, God. Keep your hands wrapped around us; hold us together. Tear open the sky and come! "Come, Lord Jesus!"

Our good news text this morning, our gospel text, began with words of Jesus, about the kingdom of God.

But in those days, after the suffering, the sun will be darkened, and the moon will not give its light, and the stars will be falling from heaven, and the powers in the heavens will be shaken. Then they will see "the Son of Man coming in clouds" with great power and glory.
— Mark 13:24-26

What did Jesus mean when he said the kingdom of God was at hand? Jesus believed that God who created the universe, the God of the covenant who promised never to abandon the creation does bring love and justice, mercy and truth, to bear upon the whole world; and God will bring renewal and healing to all creation.

A number of years ago, when my children were very young, we were all home together on an Advent season mid-week evening. Early December darkness had settled in very comfortably. There was the warmth of a fire in the fireplace, lit candles, and music from the stereo. Andrew, six years old at the time, pulled a jigsaw puzzle box out of the hall closet and dumped its contents on the coffee table by the fireplace. The picture on the puzzle was of an American cult object. It was a photograph of the defensive line of the Dallas Cowboys in action. (This was back when Dallas dominated the NFL.) The picture was of Too Tall Jones and his teammates in the process of sacking Craig Morton. The puzzle pieces were an array of color: bright Denver red and Dallas blue with the blur of fans in the stadium in the background — a challenging puzzle! All four of us had to work on this one.

First the rectangular border was completed, and then inner sections of the puzzle began to take ragged bites out of the white marble top of the table. It was all coming together. After a long time, finally the end was near. We could feel it. There was a certain tension in the air. Shirley, Andrew, and I hovered over the table. There was no time for conversation now. One hand for the puzzle and one hand for the popcorn. Salty, buttered fingers were flying fast as the pieces were fitted into place. Andrew, at six years old, had well-developed spatial coordination and held his own. But Kirsten, barely five years old, had a trial-and-error approach that gave her limited success. At some point, she had quietly gathered colored pencils and paper and worked intently at the other end of the table, still a part of the group, in the atmosphere of community, but doing her own thing. I thought of offering her my successful puzzle discoveries to put in place, but she would have considered that condescending. I was left to watch her out of the corner of my eye and made sure she was supplied with popcorn.

At one point though, I noticed Kirsten quietly slide down to the puzzle end of the table seemingly to examine our handiwork. Then I saw her quickly, secretly, slip into the sleeve of her sweater a single piece of the puzzle, and return to her end of the table to resume her artwork.

I moved over next to her and whispered in her ear, "Kirsten, why did you take that puzzle piece?" She said simply, "I want to put a piece in, too, and if I wait until the very end, I'll know right where it goes."

The Christian confession is that the ending for which we wait is already in hand and fully present in Jesus as the Christ. Although things are not completed, we have the last piece of the puzzle already. Our Advent longing, our waiting, has taken on a new dimension. We are still a part of all creation that groans for completion and reunion. But we know now what that completion looks like — we know it in the story of Jesus.

We are between times, or better stated, at the center. We long for a final completion but now have the vision of how it all should be, and will be, in the story of Jesus. And when we tell the story of Jesus, we are doing so as part of the community that is called to model this story to the world.

Advent waiting is not just longing for some future state called "heaven," but in the light of Christ we know that God is also infused in the present world. "Thy kingdom come," said Jesus, "thy will be done, on earth as it is in heaven." It is the desire for things to be made right here and now, as well as in the end.

Jesus guided listeners to come to terms with God's reality breaking in to their midst, and helped them to do and be what they longed for. Jesus announced a new context and challenged his hearers to become the new people that this new context demanded, the citizens of this new world. He was offering a challenge to his contemporaries to a way of life, a way of forgiveness and prayer and giving and acceptance, which they could practice in their own villages, right where they were. They could not only talk about God's mending of the creation, but, also, contribute to that mending and to raise up signs of new creation in our teaching, writing, work, and play.

We still live in the Advent season. We are still waiting. But in Christ we know what we await. Scriptural apocalyptic confessions should inspire us to declare that the reality and revelation of Christ is the hope of the whole world. And it is the duty of believers to live out that reality now, wide-awake, and in celebration of that promised completion.

Amen. "Come Lord, Jesus."

Sermon delivered November 28, 1999
First Lutheran Church
Duluth, Minnesota

Advent 2
Isaiah 11:1-10; Matthew 3:1-12

Mother Teresa And The Messianic Life

*"On that day," promised wild Isaiah, "on that day when
things are finally set right, the wolf shall live with the
lamb, the calf and the lion together, the cow and the
bear will graze together, the time of violence will be
over, God's harmony will prevail. On that day there
will be peace — when the true 'anointed one' rules —
when the genuine Messiah comes; it will be 'God with
us' — Immanuel — peace, at last."*
— Isaiah 11:1-10 cf

*A voice cries in the wilderness, "Prepare now the way
for the Lord; clear a straight path for him." John the
Baptist proclaimed, "I baptize you with water, for re-
pentance; but the one who comes directly after me is
mightier than I am, whose sandals I am not worthy to
remove. He will baptize you with the Holy Spirit and
with fire."* — Matthew 3:11 cf

It will be the Messiah who will bring in the kingdom of God,
the Christ.

I read of a rabbi who said, "I do not believe Jesus was the
Messiah not because I do not believe in the Messiah, but because
Jesus did not bring the messianic age." The prophets longed for the
advent of the Messiah, the day of the Lord when the just would be
vindicated and the unjust judged fairly, that time of pure shalom
when the lion and lamb would lie down together, when war would
cease, human abuse would be banished, and environmental degra-
dation ended. Well, obviously, post-Christmas, and post Easter, this
has not happened.

Just before last Thanksgiving I had an opportunity to spend a few hours in one of my favorite places — the Philadelphia Museum of Art — where I became reacquainted with some of my favorite paintings. This museum has an extensive collection of the work of Edward Hicks, a Quaker preacher who also painted in the early 1800s. Hicks is perhaps best known for his series of paintings titled *The Peaceable Kingdom* that he based on the theme and hope of this morning's reading from Isaiah. In the foreground of these paintings are the symbols of Isaiah's vision of shalom under the reign of God: a lion and lamb lying down together, a bear with a cow, and a snake with a child. In the background of these paintings, standing along the banks of the Delaware River, is William Penn greeting Native American chieftains. They have come together to ratify an agreement of peace in which they all pledge to respect each other and share the wonders of this land, which for Penn was a new land, a bountiful frontier of possibilities, a new beginning, a new Eden. Hicks' paintings are the artwork of great hope and expectations — a hope for a new world, a new start — the messianic age at last. "Prepare ye the way of the Lord!"

Broken treaties and clear-cut forests soon destroyed the tranquility of such a great and immanent expectation. The paintings quickly became symbols pointing again to future hope for a messianic age.

Last spring break, my son, Andrew, and I spent a day at the Met in New York while they were featuring the work of the artist, Horace Pippin. Horace Pippin, born in 1888, spent most of his life in New Jersey working as a young man in a coal yard and an iron foundry. Then he worked as a hotel porter and a used-clothing peddler. In 1917, the 29-year-old enlisted and served in the war in an all African-American Infantry Regiment. He was shot through the right shoulder by a German sniper and honorably discharged. He married a woman who worked in a laundry. As therapy for his injured arm, which he could no longer raise above shoulder height, Pippin began using charcoal to decorate discarded cigar boxes. It went from there to painting with his right hand propped up by his left, and he was eventually "discovered"! His depictions of African-American mothers lovingly bathing their children on Saturday night, serving them breakfast on Christmas morning, and presiding over their evening prayers, were sought out by major museums. Along with these scenes of family harmony were also paintings portraying death in war, and racial prejudice in this country; for example, there was a painting of a Klansman watching black and white soldiers being forced apart.

The most haunting painting by Pippin on display at the Met that day was where Pippen put both themes together — war and peace. It was titled *The Holy Mountain*. Pippen wrote about this painting: "... one thinks of peace ... can there be peace, yes there will be peace, so I looked at Isaiah 11:6-10. I went over it four or five times in my mind. Every time I read it I got a new thought on it. So I went to work."

In the foreground, living in peaceful co-habitation, are the lamb and the lion, the bear and the cow, the leopard and the goat, and a young child is leading them. But in the background, in the shadows of the forest, there are scenes of combat, tanks and soldiers, and there is a lynching, and a row of graves. The painting was completed on August 9 — the day the Americans dropped the atomic bomb on Nagasaki.

What kind of messianic hope is this? In the background the human lion still devours the lamb if given the opportunity; our life together is marked by a constant stream of injustice, but Pippin, a devout Christian, saw something else already occurring in the foreground of our lives — a messianic gift, already given and by some, received and accepted. Immanuel.

I am going to tell you a true story. One summer I was in Calcutta, India, in July. It was an arena of incredible heat and dust, and a feeling that all of humanity had somehow managed to gather together in this one location and form one pulsing community of flesh and blood in action. There was a flow of people interwoven with the smoke of cooking fires and the sound of the traffic — a parade of life stepping over others — sleeping, praying, eating, and dying.

At the time I was running a very high fever, trying to find boiled or carbonated liquids to force down, trying to focus my eyes and hold my physical self together in the heat and dust. But when the invitation came to encounter a living, universal symbol of transcendent love, I was not going to ignore it. No matter how sick I was, there was so much hope and purpose packaged into that living symbol that I was invited to encounter in person, I did not want to be denied that encounter with hope. So I borrowed strength from the future and accepted the invitation to walk down the shadows of a narrow alley near a Kali temple and enter into a home for sick and abandoned babies that also served as her home. When Mother Teresa entered the room, I thought to myself, "My God, she is parchment paper, she is straw, just a fragile, frail, little human being. She is a mere candle flame in a vast hurricane of pain. My God, she is only parchment paper." Then she spoke, and I saw the fire in her eyes and experienced the power of her words and her purpose and the endlessness.

Mother Teresa may be accused of being naive. Don't ask her about the pros and cons of nuclear power plants, or about the ordination of women. Rather just sit at her feet and listen to a particularly clear expression of God's words uttered through her lips and God's eternity shining through her eyes. Most precisely, it is in her actions that one sees God. She is one who clearly lives a messianic faith now in our broken world.

Since she won the Nobel Peace Prize in 1979 there have been a large number of books and articles written about Mother Teresa, all trying to catch her spirit. But she runs so counter to the definitions of success that resonate within our society today that the essence of her personhood is hard for most to fathom. Biographers often try to find her source of power by excavating her past — her childhood, her schooling, and the years she was a high school principal, and they are surprised to find that very few people could even remember her then. Those who could remember remark only about how ordinary she was. Like a stable birth or a carpenter shop upbringing — it all lacks the trappings of power.

Interviews of Mother Teresa by the secular media often go unheard, not broadcast or published because she speaks very simply using the language of the church and the scriptures — a language and a moral sensitivity that has shriveled in today's often self-centered secular society, a society that no longer takes seriously the concept of the incarnation and that has real difficulty comprehending the thought and life of those who do. But I have come across an essay concerning a dialogue that Malcolm Muggeridge had with Mother Teresa, and which, from my point of view, catches the transcendence of this fragile woman. Muggeridge, who wrote *The Third Testament*, said to her, "Our fellow human beings, or many of them, perhaps including myself, have lost their way. You have found the way. How do you help them find the way?" Her simple answer, "By getting them in touch with people, for in people they will find God."

Muggeridge knew how most of our contemporaries would take that answer. To suggest to many a college student or faculty member that the people he or she meets every day would be central to salvation seems like nonsense. So Muggeridge pushed her to articulate her faith, not just live it. "You mean," he asked with mock incredulity, "that the road to faith and the road to God is via our fellow human beings"? She replied, "Because we cannot see Christ, we cannot express our love to him, but our neighbors we can always see, and we can do to them what if we saw Christ we would like to do to him ... in the slums, in the broken bodies, in the children, we see Christ and we touch him."

She was asked, "Aren't there already too many people in India? I mean, is it worth salvaging a few abandoned children who might otherwise eventually die anyway?" She could not comprehend the question. From our sophisticated, calculated growth-profit oriented point of view, such incomprehension betrays an inability to think beyond one's own values and to grasp ideas impersonally and objectively. She would probably flunk out of Wittenberg University. "Is it worth salvaging a few abandoned children?" For her, this is a question of madness. *All* life is sacred. She could only stammer — "I believe in love and compassion."

The message of John the Baptist, in this morning's gospel text, is that Mother Teresa is not a remnant of a simpler time or simpler mindset, but she is a manifestation of the new age, the new person who accepts the reality of incarnation, who lives the light of Immanuel — God with us — right now.

41

During the civil war that gutted Lebanon, Mother Teresa went to Beirut after a major shelling. She was in the streets helping place two wounded children into an ambulance when she was accosted by several Western reporters. One of the reporters asked her if she thought her relief effects could be considered successful given the fact that there were 100 other children in a nearby, bombed-out hospital whom she wasn't helping. She replied, "Don't you think it is a good thing to help these little ones?" The reporter did not flinch but asked his question again. "The other hospital has many wounded children, too. Can you call your efforts successful if you leave them unattended?" Mother Teresa sighed and answered her own question, "I think it is a good thing to help these children." Then her shoulder sank beneath the weight of the stretcher.

The incarnation of divine love, transcends time and flows in opposition to the systems of human power and glory, and cuts through the legalisms of our communal living.

That summer of my Indian pilgrimage, it wasn't the fever that caused me to see the incarnate Christ in the light emanating from the soul of that small, parchment-paper body in the heat and dust of Calcutta. It wasn't the fever, when I saw the peaceable kingdom in the laughter of now plump children held by the nuns in her clinic. It wasn't the fever, when I saw the lion and the lamb together in her home for the dying — as a British physician embraced an elderly woman who was breathing her last breath, but now held in the arms of compassion. It wasn't the fever; it was divine love and power active now in our time and space. It was, and is, messianic.

Come, O come, Emmanuel.

A voice cries in the wilderness, "Prepare the way of the Lord; clear a straight path for him ... He will baptize you with the Holy Spirit and with a fire ... that can never be put out."   — Matthew 3:3 cf

On that day the root of Jesse shall stand as a signal to the peoples; the nations shall inquire of him, and his dwelling shall be glorious.   — Isaiah 11:10

Not yet, but already now. Today is also "that day — the root of Jesse shall stand as a signal to all the people."

Sermon delivered December 10, 1995
Weaver Chapel
Wittenberg University
Springfield, Ohio

The article from which the material about Mother Teresa was taken appears online at http://www.religion-online.org/showarticle.asp?title=1918.

Advent 2
Matthew 3:1-12

John The Baptist And Jewel Cave

> *In those days John the Baptist appeared in the wilderness of Judea, proclaiming, "Prepare ye the way of the Lord."*
> — Matthew 1, 3 cf

The confession of the gospel story is that the Lord did come; that the long-awaited Messiah did come in Jesus! But what difference does that make?

One summer when my children were in elementary school, our family of four went for a summer camping vacation. One of our stops was Jewel Cave in South Dakota. Jewel Cave is a designated National Monument, and the cave itself contains over 100 kilometers of surveyed passageways. We signed up for a walking tour led by a naturalist/ranger that went through some sections of the cave that are not normally visited by tourists. The regular visitors walk through so-called "improved" passageways where the cave floor has been smoothed out, railings and steps added, and the chambers illuminated like an airport runway. But in the cave portions of our guided walk, there was no electricity. We all carried old-style candle lanterns through "unimproved" passageways; in other words, we stumbled around together in the dark.

Actually it was a wonderful experience, full of wonders. It had been a hot day up on the prairie, but underground it was refreshingly cool, and the pure quiet of the place was so very obvious. We made the only sounds. We generated the only light. The various stalactites and stalagmites and columns seemed to animate in our lantern light, and the domes and pits appeared to be endless; the only appreciable life was contained within us, our small caravan of travelers walking carefully together on unsure footing.

At one point our guide told us to bring our lanterns together and hold them high, and he pointed to a large accretion on the cave ceiling. The formation stood out, tall and softly, smoothly rounded. The lanterns generated a host of shadows that made it appear as though the formation was rhythmically moving as though it was breathing, or slightly rocking back and forth as if tired of remaining in that same position for so long, for so many eons. The guide said that the early cave explorers named this formation "The Madonna and Child." And yes, you could see the form "The Madonna and Child." A father in our group bent low and whispered to his ten-year-old daughter, "that means it looks like a mother and a baby." The light of my lantern just caught the girl's smile as her eyes widened in recognition.

Kirsten, my daughter, who was entering first grade in the fall, tugged at my sleeve, her fear of the dark abated for the moment, and she said to me, "It's Mary and Baby Jesus!"

Our naturalist/guide mumbled something about the formation being "calcite crystals and large hydromagnesite bubbles."

And then we turned our lanterns away and stumbled down a different passageway over the rubble, and the formation on the ceiling returned to the dark stillness of its limestone chamber.

Isn't that the story of our human journey as we stumble through life together — looking for the guide, hoping the light doesn't go out, hopefully holding hands for assurance and protection?

Does it make a difference whether our life experience includes Baby Jesus? Does Jesus make a difference in our living?

For many the birth of this baby is overlooked as just another expression of the natural process in some ultimately meaningless flow of life; Jesus is just one more person.

For others, that birth is only viewed sentimentally; as an example of the miracle of birth; the Christmas image of a helpless, innocent child protected and nurtured by a loving parent; parental hope passed on from generation to generation. And babies are cute, even a human baby lying in an animal manger.

But for Christians there is a faith confession that says out loud that this is "Mary and Baby Jesus." This is the long-awaited

Messiah who guides us through the darkness and rubble of the journey toward the center of meaning.

> *In those days John the Baptist appeared in the wilderness of Judea, proclaiming, "Repent for the kingdom of heaven has come near." ... "Prepare ye the way of the Lord" ... "I baptize you with water for repentance, but one who is more powerful than I is coming after me; I am not worthy to carry his sandals. He will baptize you with the Holy Spirit and fire."*
>
> — Matthew 3:1-3, 11

The confession of the church is that this Savior did come — in the person of Jesus! But what difference does that coming make? Was not God there, and active in human history and hope before Jesus of Nazareth? Was not God interactive and present after Jesus of Nazareth? What difference does it make — this birth for which we wait in these days of Advent preparation and hope?

The Christian confession is that it makes all the difference in the world!

Two weeks ago, I attended the annual meeting of the American Academy of Religion, of which I am a member. We met concurrently with the Society for Biblical Literature. Gathered in one location were hundreds and hundreds of religion, theology, and biblical professors and scholars from this country and others from around the world. There were over 650 seminars, lectures, and formal gatherings offered during the four-day conference on such topics as: "Syntactic Aspects of Co-ordinate Subjects with Independent Personal Pronouns in Biblical Hebrew" and "The UFO Cult and the Meaning of Life." I passed up those two, but one of the sessions I did attend was a panel discussion of biblical scholars on the topic of the historical Jesus.

Biblical scholars like to make a distinction between the pre-Easter Jesus and the post-Easter Jesus. The pre-Easter Jesus is the historical Jesus, the person you could touch and talk with if you could be transported back in time to Palestine in the years 20 to 30 AD.

The post-Easter Jesus is the Christ that the later church lifted up and continued to experience. It is the victorious Christ. For example, if you enter old Greek or Russian Orthodox churches, and look up at the central icon painted on the dome, you find Jesus as *Christus Victor* — the victorious Christ over all the universe. In some churches it is the image of Christ as the final judge at heaven's gate. It is the post-Easter Christ who encounters and engages us today. But what about the person who was born into poverty, who walked through the fields and flowers along the banks of the Sea of Galilee, who preached in local houses and synagogues, and was executed in Jerusalem?

Does the pre-Easter Jesus matter for Christianity and the church? For centuries upon centuries, the church knew only the post-Easter Jesus and was engaged by the Spirit and peace of God. They were grasped by faith. It has only been in the last few decades that we have probed scripture and archeological evidence with a scientific eye to seek out in more detail the historical person of Jesus.

One panel member, Marcus Borg, a Lutheran, said that if we don't attempt to discover and study and discuss the historical Jesus today, we are at risk of losing both the pre-Easter and the post-Easter Jesus because they define each other. John Dominic Crossan, a Roman Catholic scholar, said that historical research on Jesus is essential for evangelism today. As we share the faith, we should carefully make distinctions between the historical evidence, and the symbolic and theological statements and stories that are also held within the Bible. Making such distinctions, while seeking the truth in each, liberates us from a literalistic interpretation of the text and therefore a possible misinterpretation of the text's original meaning.

For example, when we study the historical Jesus, it becomes obvious how much Jesus was directly involved in the political events of his day, challenging the authorities to heed the call from God to bring about justice and peace, caring for the ill, accepting the rejected, and calling all people into a loving community. For here we can see God's actions among us.

Jesus takes the insights and images of his religious culture, and lives out the answer to such questions as, "What does the wisdom of God look like?" Look at Jesus! "What does the embodiment of the 'Word of God' or the 'passion of God' do in the world?" Look at Jesus! "What would it look like if the hope of the prophet Isaiah for a world at peace were to come true?" Look at Jesus! "What form does the grace of God take in human interactions before the final judgment?" Look at Jesus!

By examining the historical Jesus, it helps us to envision what it means to be a Christian today, and what would God do if God entered into our workplace or worship service. What would Jesus do or say? Those bracelets that so many youth wear today with the initials WWJD — "What would Jesus do?" — are right on target, I believe. "What would Jesus do?" is the right question if one has studied carefully and knows both at once — the pre-Easter Jesus and the resurrected Lord.

As Advent people, we await the Christmas coming of Jesus which we claim is an encounter with God. The historical Jesus tells us that the Creator God is a God of love. The pre-Easter Jesus and the risen Lord are one in Jesus Christ. And it makes all the difference in the world!

The Lutheran theologian, Carl Braaten, wrote, "Because of the real humanity of God in Christ, the wall of separation between the Holy and the common, between the religious and the secular, between the soul and the body, between the world now and the one to come, between history and eschatology, between the natural and the supernatural — the perceived barrier separating each of these pairs has been shattered" by Jesus. Jesus gives a center for all our living.

Advent time is waiting for the birth of a real baby — Baby Jesus as one of us but, also, as Christ the Lord — the touch point with God now and our future with God. Advent is a time to be ready and open to the fact that our Lord is being born in our midst in all the situations of life that demand our love, our acceptance, and the giving of ourselves.

The past four days I was pastor-in-residence at Concordia College in Moorhead, Minnesota. The chapel ministry program at

Concordia had a poster that they put on bulletin boards around campus. The poster stated: "Without God, it is a vicious circle." Jesus, as the Christ, ends the vicious circle. And this makes all the difference in the world.

"In those days John the Baptist appeared in the wilderness of Judea, proclaiming, 'Prepare the way of the Lord' " (Matthew 1, 3 cf).

It makes all the difference in the world.

Sermon delivered December 6, 1998
First Lutheran Church
Duluth, Minnesota

Combat Fatigue And Christmas

Be patient, my brothers, until the Lord comes. The farmer looking for the precious crop his land may yield can only wait in patience, until the winter and spring rains have fallen. You too must be patient and stout-hearted, for the coming of the Lord is near.

— James 5:7-9 cf

Three verses from James 5, from today's second lesson. Waiting, in patience, has always had a theological significance even though, I am sure at first thought, waiting means people queuing up at a cash register in a supermarket or Christmas-decorated department store, or waiting for a sermon to be over. But waiting is far more significant. It is a part of being human; waiting is at the heart of religion and meaning. Let me give some quick examples from history.

A representative example of "waiting" at the dawn of civilization would be in the annual spring festival held in ancient Egypt as early as 3000 BC.

In the vast majority of early civilizations, it was agriculture that gave life, and the gods were of rain and sun and soil. A person's religion consisted of year after year waiting patiently and hopefully for the gods to bless them with rain and satisfactory growing weather or curse them with drought or storm.

The Egyptian spring festival celebrated the death and resurrection of the god Osiris. A model of the dead god was cast in a gold mold in the form of a hollow mummy and then filled with a mixture of barley and sand; it was wrapped in rushes and laid in a shallow container. For nine days the people watered this idol and waited. On the tenth day it was exposed to the sun. And the people waited.

On the fourteenth day this gold mummy god was placed in a coffin and buried in a grave. On the nineteenth and the last day of the festival, the god Osiris was pulled out of the grave — out of the ground. It was for them an annual resurrection of the god; it was like wheat growing from the soil.

The festival was timed to correspond with the Nile River returning to its banks after its annual flooding, after bringing new moist soil; and on the last day of the festival, as Osiris is pulled from the earth, the people go to their fields to see what they were waiting for — their newly sown grain sprouting from the moist soil. It was a waiting for life.

A carving in an ancient Egyptian temple shows stalks of wheat growing from the mummy of the dead god watered by a priest from a pitcher. By the mummy is an inscription that reads, "This is the form of him who may not be named, Osiris of the mysteries who springs from the returning waters."

The people's long winter wait is fulfilled but not totally, because there will be another year and they will wait and worry again if the god will rise and if the grain will grow.

This mentality is typical of early civilization and religions. Usually the waiting was even more critical because most rains and rivers were not as dependable as the Nile. But in each situation, waiting was necessary for life.

Let me use another typical example from history, this time about 3,000 years later, and look at gnosticism in the ancient Near East and Roman world.

Gnosticism had many different forms, but its primary concern was one of waiting — a waiting for the spirit of god to come and reveal "truth," to reveal ultimate "knowledge" or "gnosis" to an individual.

Gnostics believed god was good, was truth, and was light and that the world was bad, was false, and was darkness. The world was like a vast prison whose innermost dungeon was the earth. In the cosmos that separates god from earth there were believed to be lesser demon gods who ruled the world and stopped any interaction between god and earth.

Humans were a part of the evil world but encased in each person was a spirit, a *pneuma*, which was a portion of the divine substance — a piece of goodness that had fallen into the world.

This spirit of god immersed in flesh, was stupefied, asleep, or intoxicated by the poison of the world; it was ignored and could only be awakened and liberated by the coming of "knowledge" or "truth." So the gnostic waited.

The gnostic waited for a messenger from the world of light to penetrate the barrier of the spheres and earth, and outwit the guardian, evil gods, and awaken the inner spirit of a person from its earthly slumber and give it saving knowledge.

Gnostics waited for a messenger, a messenger to give them the key to life. They waited and waited.

In all cases, humanity senses that it requires waiting for total life. But whether you are waiting for the right thing or not is another question.

It is no different today, no matter what level you wait.

I read in a magazine that every once in a while the local people on one island of the New Hebrides in the South Pacific paint their bodies with red paint to spell out the letters USA and, equipped with bamboo poles to symbolize rifles, they march down to the shores of the Pacific to await the arrival of John Frum.

John Frum is a legendary soldier who they expect to reappear from the surf in landing crafts filled with the Jeeps and chewing gum and the other marvels of industrialized society that the GIs brought to the New Hebrides during World War II. They wait patiently for this, for what they consider an advanced form of life, but John Frum never comes.

Also in New Guinea, I believe, backwoods tribes now and then carve airplane runways out of the jungle and sit and wait for the giant WWII cargo planes to return. They call them "giant bird gods from the sky." They wait but nothing happens.

Waiting is a part of being human. We all wait for life, for meaning, and for what we see as ultimately important. All people wait, but what they're waiting for is often quite different.

Communists classically wait and work for the final synthesis when conflict will end in equality. Buddhists classically wait with life and fulfillment, then they wait for that big winning lottery ticket or that long shot horse to win big, or to guess the bottom of the stock market.

It's waiting — but waiting for what? And if what you are waiting for comes, will it fulfill?

Waiting means not having and having at the same time. The condition of man's relation to God is first of all one of not having, not seeing, not knowing, and not grasping. Religion in which this is forgotten replaces God by its own creation. Some people don't wait for God because they say they possess him totally in a book — the Bible — or in an institution — a church or temple. They possess him in their own experience.

You cannot possess God if he is the true power of life. It's hard to proclaim God to children or pagans or skeptics or secularists and at the same time make clear to them that we don't possess God, that we, too, wait for him.

The theologian, Paul Tillich, once wrote that much of the rebellion against Christianity was due to Christian's covert or veiled claim to possess God already and therefore have no need to wait.

Is God a thing that can be grasped and known among other things? Is God less than a human person? We always have to wait for a human being. Even in the most intimate communion among human beings, there is an element of not having and not knowing, and of waiting.

Although waiting is not having, it is also in a sense having. The fact that we wait for something shows that in some way we are already grasped by it. If we wait in hope and patience, the power of that for which we wait is already effective within us.

One who waits in an ultimate sense is not far from that for which he waits. One who waits in absolute seriousness is already grasped by that for which he waits.

One who waits in patience has already received the power of that for which he waits. One who waits passionately is already an active power himself.

The key, though, is what are you waiting for — for rain, for an idol of gold, money, or power. Christianity describes our existence in relation to God as one of waiting also, but waiting for one who directs in love and whom we, as Christians, say fulfills all life. Our waiting is not one of despair or emptiness.

All time runs forward. All time, both in history and in personal life, is expectation. Time itself is waiting, not for another time, but for that which is eternal.

It is December 15. We are in the process of waiting for Christmas. After almost two months of an unremitting heavy-artillery promotional barrage in advertising in stores and the media, we are in a state of combat fatigue, if not bankruptcy, by December 25.

We are almost tired of waiting, but waiting for Christmas is essential. It permits us, compels us, to take seriously the reality of our present situation. We don't live in a world of perpetual Christmas mornings. We live in a Maundy Thursday to Good Friday world. We are waiting in a world where some people don't trust each other or love each other much, where peace on earth and goodwill to people are at times hard to find.

After almost 2,000 Christmas mornings, Christians still find it hard to be fully human and honest, free and responsive, even within the close circles of our own families or church friends, let alone the wider circle of humanity.

But in this waiting for the coming, in this wait for the Advent, we can also participate in the Christ we hope for. Christmas is not to be a winter-wonderland orgy of escapism, but it is a festival of light in darkness.

In waiting, we can recognize the darkness — our darkness — and also see the coming of light in God's love through Christ.

Having to wait is not a curse but a gift of time to discover meaning: time to write a loving card to a friend, time to read, to pray, to find someone whose Christmas would be lost without you, time to care, time to prepare for the coming of the Lord, time to sense that God knows when and where he will be born into our lives.

This is the eternal message of Advent, of waiting for Christmas: time to watch and pray. Advent is time to be ready and open to perceive that our Lord is being born in our midst in all the situations of life that demand our love, our acceptance, and our giving of ourselves; it's our Christmas present here and now.

We have waiting time to sense that God is alive and at hand, that the power of life is beginning to act now in our lives and in the lives of all his people to bring light in our darkness.

Sermon delivered December 21, 1997
First Lutheran Church
Duluth, Minnesota

Mary, The Mother Of Jesus

"Hail Mary, full of grace...."

*And Mary said, "My soul magnifies the Lord, and my
spirit rejoices in God my Savior."*   — Luke 1:46-47

It is not unusual to encounter media news articles reporting, with a smile, an alleged appearance of Mary occurring usually in some economically depressed location. Perhaps Mary was sighted at a small, ramshackle farm in Convers, Georgia, for example, her image miraculously appearing on a red-stained side of a barn, or perhaps in the night sky above a trailer park outside of Denver. Traffic jams may occur for a day or so as the faithful or curious flock to see the alleged phenomenon.

What is unusual though, is how rarely Mary actually appears in the pages of our Bible. The apostle Paul never mentions Mary's name. Mark's gospel skips the birth of Jesus and, later, along with the gospel of John, portrays Mary as a person who really doesn't understand the mission of her son. But in the gospel of Luke, Mary sings a poem that focuses not on herself but on her God. Here we clearly find blessed Mary full of grace, the holy mother of our Lord and Savior, Jesus Christ.

"My soul magnifies the Lord ..." Mary's song, later named the "Magnificat" from its opening word in the Latin Vulgate, God is magnified — it is easier now to see the divine. Mary's song tells of a God who has "looked with favor on [her] lowliness" (Luke 1:48), the Greek pointing not just to her humility, but to her economic position, her low status in her culture, her material poverty like many pregnant teenagers in our own urban and rural areas today. Mary was a member of the Palestinian underclass, and yet a woman who knows God and is therefore blessed. "My spirit rejoices in God my savior...." It is Mary who sings the "freedom song" on behalf of all those who have their priorities tied to the agenda of God, many of whom are very poor.

Martin Luther was nurtured in a spiritual environment that included the cult of Mary in both personal piety and liturgical expression. Because of the Magnificat, Luther considered Mary a primary symbol of the embodiment of God's unmerited grace. In Mary, Luther saw true reverence as opposed to the arrogance of worldly power. He saw Mary as the prototype of how God is to be *magnified* by Christians, not praised for distant, unchangeable majesty but for the unconditional, graceful, and loving pursuit of all the earth's sacred life. Mary magnifies God for what God does rather than magnifying herself or what God has done for her alone. The only Lutheran-reformational warning concerning Mary was that we should never confuse Mary for Mary's God.

I firmly believe Mary has much to teach us today about the nature of God. I will offer one sermon illustration this morning. It is a true story about an alleged appearance of the Virgin Mary — an appearance story that, I believe, nicely exposes the very nature of God.

The story takes place in Mexico in the early 1500s. It begins on the top of a hill that just a few years before was a pilgrimage center of the Aztec religion. It was the location of a temple to an awesome and greatly feared Aztec goddess dressed in her "star skirt" representing power over the whole universe. The temple had recently been destroyed by the Spanish Conquistadors. It was precisely on that hill during this time of year in December, according to tradition, that Mary appeared to an American Indian peasant with the baptismal name of Juan Diego. The year was 1531. Mary appeared to Juan Diego and told him that a church should be built on that site and that he was to convince the Spanish Bishop of Mexico to build it.

The Indian was instructed by Mary to pick roses of Castile, which he would find growing in the December desert nearby and carry them in his *tilma*, his rough, native cloak, to the bishop in Mexico City.

Juan Diego followed Mary's instructions, but when the Indian knelt before the skeptical bishop and opened his poncho to offer the roses, the flowers were gone. On his robe was a painting of Mary, painted right on the course, indigenous cloth woven of local plant fibers — the cloth of the Aztec. This painting of Mary, a gift from Mary, as many believe, has been named *Our Lady of Guadalupe*, and it has been the focus of Mexican religious life for over 400 years.

But this story is not just about an alleged miracle. It is about human beings encountering God through an understanding of Mary, the mother of Jesus. Come deeper with me into this tradition, beginning with the Conquistadors. I am certainly not trying to make excuses for much of what they did, which was often brutal injustice stemming from pure cultural and racial prejudice and misunderstanding, but I want to first attempt to understand their perception of Mary. Remember that most of these soldiers were from the poorest levels of Spanish society, desperately entering the military, and, for the most part, they were genuinely religious people.

The soldiers' theology tended toward apocalyptic. They envisioned themselves on the edge of chaos, facing death each day in a land they knew nothing about. In fact, just a few years before, it was a land not even believed to exist. They were in alien territory and the Aztecs were radically different. The Spanish soldiers, who were appalled by the ritual blood-letting, self-mutilation, and human sacrifice of the Aztec religion, wondered if the native peoples might be devils. "Will they kill me? Will I ever get home to Spain again? The odds are all against my survival!" these soldiers assumed.

But for them, Mary was also there with them. The Spanish soldiers all carried images of Mary wherever they went. She was a symbol to them that God would not forget them or abandon them even in this new, bizarre, and hostile world. Even if they would die a violent death so far from home, they would die in the arms of Mary, and would not be Godforsaken. Mary was like their own mother, or the mother they wished they would have had, a mother who knew their suffering and would never forget them. It was, I believe, a valid image of God — the mother's caring love and long memory. But the soldiers often grossly missed the other primary component of the Magnificat — the part about justice and loving your neighbor as yourself.

But what about the Aztecs?

At first, for both those who allied themselves with or battled against the Spaniards in 1519 through 1521, the so-called "years of the conquest," images of Mary were associated with terror and pain. During that time, Cortes and his troops conspicuously carried pictures and banners of Mary everywhere, even into battle. According to Spanish records, they placed statues of Mary in the native temples after they were cleansed of their "pagan idols" (the words used in the journals of the Spanish officers). After the battle of Tabasco, for example, the conquered Aztec chiefs who were still alive were instructed in the basic beliefs of Christianity while seated before an image of Mary holding the Christ Child. So for the Aztecs, Mary, at first, must have been viewed as the harbinger of death, destruction, and humiliation.

The pre-Columbian Aztec religion was, at its core, apocalyptic — a delicate balance of life and death. Human sacrifice, that so horrified the Spaniards, was a part of that perceived balance — sacrifice was necessary — for life demands death so that more could live. There must be death if there is to be life — and so there were ornate ceremonies and rules to keep to maintain the balance; if not they would be punished by angry gods. The Spanish conquest upset this delicate balance and tipped the Aztec perception of meaning into chaos. Many Indians died in battles, and most — millions — died in the epidemics of the mid-1500s and later. The destruction of their temples also lead Indians to despair ... the old gods that maintained the balance were swept away, and the native people believed they were observing the death of the world. Right after the conquest (their holocaust) many of the Aztec survivors refused to have children — why bring children into a dead world? Many Aztecs committed suicide. Their culture was in its death throes. Then there was a miracle, they believed. Mary came to them in an image on their own woven, Aztec cloth — *Our Lady of Guadalupe.*

In that painting, Mary wore a dress that seemed to be covered with stars (a blue dress with white dotted highlights was common in many European paintings of Mary at the time) — but in Mexico it was, for the Indians, the "star-skirt" previously worn by Aztec goddesses who watched over the daily routine of birth, life, and death. This Mary knew their story — their beliefs; this woman was one of them ... they believed. And she was the mother of Jesus.

This added a new insight into the divine nature of things — the tenuous balance between life and ravenous death that had demanded fear and a hierarchy of power from kings to slaves. It added a new insight into the necessity to spill blood in mutilation, sacrifice, and war to sustain life — causing death! This cosmology was altered when they viewed life through the eyes of Mary and her song, the Magnificat.

Rather than death holding the final word, life in compassionate community was now perceived to be the ultimate victor through the gift of God's love — an engaging love that also called for justice in regard to the Spanish occupation, which reminded them of the Roman occupation in the Bible. The suffering of war, death, and disease was real and horrible but not what God intended. And the God of Mary did know their suffering — her own, beloved son was unjustly brutalized and killed. Mary could cry with them ... yet also gently assist them into the realization that these injustices of life need not lead to despair, nor are they God's will, nor are they the final word. "You are sacred," Mary told them. "You are highly valued by God who wills life — your life ... and compassionate life in all its wholeness."

I don't think the Spanish or their organized church in Mexico at the time knew exactly what was happening, but I do believe that the image of Mary in that situation enabled the Advent of Christ. That image revealed the actuality and the love of God, as defined by Jesus, offering a healing, restorative word to the suffering remnant of the Aztec civilization. Mary returned dignity without the fear, and defined a call for freedom and equality. That voice of God, through Mary, still wishes to speak to us.

Martin Luther preached the following in a Christmas sermon.

"For unto you is born this day." For our sakes he has taken flesh and blood from a woman, that his birth might become our birth. I, too, may boast that I am a son of Mary. This is the way to observe this feast — that Christ be formed in us. It is not enough that we should hear his story if the heart be closed. I must listen, not to a history, but to a gift. If you hear that this Child is yours, and that takes root, you will become suddenly so strong that to you death and life are the same.

In other words, Mary makes clear the feminine aspect of God — of God aware of our suffering — of absolutely knowing our pain and inner desires — a loving mother — Mary as caretaker and comforter, and a clear call for liberation and peace.

In the Magnificat, Mary sings of the distinction between wisdom and might, between selfish use of riches and power on the one side and kindness, justice, and righteousness on the other. One must wonder what influence this woman had on her son — a son who later reached out to touch and heal lepers, who defended and lifted up the poor, who called the wealthy to accountability and responsibility, and who challenged all authorities concerning their use and abuse of power. She was a servant of God. Blessed Mary, full of grace, the mother of our Lord, who sang, "My soul magnifies the Lord, and my spirit rejoices in God my Savior."

And Mary remained with Elizabeth about three months, and then returned to her home in Galilee. And at that time, a decree went out from Caesar Augustus that all the world should be enrolled. This was the first registration, in the days when Quirinius was governor of Syria. All went to their own towns to be registered. Joseph went from the town of Nazareth in Galilee to Judea, to the city of David called Bethlehem ... He went to be registered with Mary, to whom he was engaged and who was expecting a child.... — Luke 1:56; 2:1-5 cf

Come, Lord Jesus ... into our homes and hearts, "Come, oh, come, Emmanuel" — God with us.

Sermon delivered December 21, 1997
First Lutheran Church
Duluth, Minnesota

Thin Places

Joseph also went [to] Bethlehem to be registered with Mary, to whom he was engaged and who was expecting a child. And while they were there, the time came for her to deliver her child. And Mary gave birth to her firstborn son and wrapped him in bands of cloth, and laid him in a manger [an animal feed box], because there was no place for them in the inn.
— Luke 2:4-7

And a holy messenger from God — an angel — appeared to poor shepherds — like us — in the darkness of the night, living out their lives, hoping their investments pay off — that their sheep will give birth. And the angel came to them, and said, "Fear not, for see, I am bringing you good news of great joy for all people."
— Luke 2:10 cf

But you know the story! At least some of the signs and symbols woven into this ancient narrative hold power and meaning for you. And the truth delicately balanced within the words of this story is what centers everything for you — enlightening all that you do. "To you is born this day in the city of David a Savior ..." (Luke 2:11).

Earlier in the fall, I received a curious request. It was from a concerned stranger. She said that the *Duluth News-Tribune*, again this year, was going to offer to local schools a special "educational section" of the paper; actually a mini-newspaper containing articles about different winter holiday celebrations. Elementary school teachers can order copies for each child in their classes for use in those last few days of school before Christmas break when students are restless and in need of something novel to keep their attention.

Here is some curriculum offered to help students learn about other customs and cultures. As the newspaper put it, your "Students should be encouraged to study and practice the traditions unique to their own families while being tolerant and knowledgeable about the beliefs and practices different from their own ... The songs, games, legends, and food associated with each celebration are excellent ways to experience other cultures."

It all sounded good to me. In the supplement were brief articles and pictures on various winter celebrations, some ancient, such as Saturnalia, a week long celebration when citizens of the Roman Empire would reflect on the beginning times when supposedly Saturn ruled the world, the good old days, when things were as they were intended to be by the gods.

The Scandinavian "Jul" was held when the pasture grasses died at the onset of winter, and some cattle were killed, and meat was momentarily plentiful, and people longed for the return of bountiful sunlight. There was an article on traditional Anishinabe or Ojibwe winter customs, many continuing today. There was information on contemporary holidays such as the ending of Ramadan for Muslims (which this year and in the next few years will occur in the winter). There were articles on Hanukkah, and on Kwanzaa, a winter celebration recalling for many African Americans their African heritage. You could read about Diwali, the harvest festival of light honoring Lakshmi, the Hindu goddess of wealth and fortune, who comes down to earth to bless the harvest.

All these brief articles were interesting and appropriate, I believe, for guided discussions in public and private classrooms to broaden perspectives in an atmosphere of learning and respect.

But, here was the concern that was brought to my attention. It was in the brief article in the paper that described the meaning of Christmas. Last year's school supplement stated something like this: "Christmas, though once a religious holiday, is now a cross-cultural celebration of gift giving and vacation time, for family gatherings and elaborate feasts." That is, of course, true! And for many of our neighbors, that is the full meaning of Christmas. But

66

isn't Christmas more than just another reason to celebrate the Winter Solstice and the return of increasing sunlight and an excuse to party? Doesn't Christmas still have a faith component, some spiritual significance for some of us today? This was the question the concerned parent who contacted me asked. Aren't we being incomplete in the education of our school children about Christmas if we don't mention what this holiday as a holy day means, for at least some people who share this complex US culture the people who attach "a confession of faith" to the celebration of Christmas?

I thought she was right, and the local editor of the school supplement agreed that there was a deficiency here. The idea for the section and much of the content originated with the *Philadelphia Inquirer*, and our local editor wondered if the Christian understanding of Christmas was ignored because Christianity is the majority religion in the United States, and therefore just about everyone already knows the biblical Christmas story and its theological significance, so there was no need to spell it out. But the truth is, many of our neighbors don't have a clue about the spiritual claims of the nativity story.

The editor at the *Duluth News-Tribune* assigned to this project was very cooperative and gracious, and agreed to at least offer equal time to Christmas. She gave me the assignment to rewrite this section on the meaning of the day for Christians, but there were some stipulations. It had to be written at a fourth-grade reading and comprehension level, for one thing. It must be understood by nine-year-olds. No big words. No complex symbols or metaphors. And I must assume that the readers have had no prior knowledge of the religious side of Christmas. I must also tell it all in no more than 350 words — a few brief paragraphs. The deadline was that same day.

How could I do this with those limitations on a topic that for me is so profoundly important, on a revelation that I believe centers our whole life, our very being? This is all so ultimately important. How do I say it all — about the birth of this baby, and say it on a fourth-grade reading level, in three or four short paragraphs?

I started by writing, "Christmas is a day when Christians celebrate the birth of Jesus Christ."

But I am already at the most important, and it often seems the most difficult, part of the story to convey to others: the meaning of the "Christ." How can I get to the heart of this right from the beginning? I recently read one description of Jesus as the Christ that I just can't use with nine-year-old kids. It is a description from Celtic Christianity. It is the concept of the "thin place."

This metaphor assumes that the reality of existence has two layers that form the whole. One, of course, is the visible world of our physical experience — the laws and processes of nature, the world of science, the measurable — cause and effect — the mechanisms of creation from evolution to heredity and DNA to global warming. The other layer that forms the whole can be called the spiritual, the source of everything, the unifying goal of all things, the final purpose, the creative intention of God, and, in classical terms, the kingdom of God!

"Thin places" are where the boundary between the two levels becomes permeable, where the boundaries separating the two become transparent and may even disappear. Jesus was a "thin place." The Christian claim is that his life — his words and actions — were a consistent and continuous point of transparency, of interaction between the world and the Spirit, between creation and the Creator, between us and God. Through the living Christ, God came and comes to us and can transform our personal lives by making us united too, complete, whole, at peace.

But how does one write about that within a culture that is so one dimensional and often incomplete and in a paragraph or two, on a fourth-grade level? I wrote, "Christmas is a day when Christians celebrate the birth of Jesus Christ. Christians believe that Jesus was 'Emmanuel' which means 'God with us all.' Jesus' words and actions always enacted God's love."

But there is so much more in the Christmas story to tell about God and the healing unity of this love. The gift of the baby in the barn is a symbol that all people are sacred, all are chosen, all are family. And incarnation means that everyday things can carry divine love, including you and me. Creation and redemption can inter-penetrate each other.

68

How was I to convey that the rejection at the inn, and the child forced into the animal feed box speaks to the destructive ways we often treat each other, and yet God still comes in love to us? How was I to make that connection, that the Christmas baby is a confession of faith that knows also crucifixion? That this incarnation — God in Jesus — is also a call to feed the hungry, clothe the naked, comfort the sorrowing, listen carefully to others in respect and love, unite divided families, establish justice, and promote peace on earth.

For fourth-grade level readers, I wrote, "Jesus was not born in a royal family but he was born in poor, humble surroundings. The story in the Bible of his birth tells us that he was born in an animal shelter. Right after his birth he was placed in the straw of a manger (an animal feeding trough) to rest. It was shepherds who came to see the baby on that first Christmas day. Because of Jesus, Christians believe that we know that God wants us to treat each other (all others) with respect and compassion."

While struggling to write this assignment, I kept hearing the words of the Christmas angel proclaiming, "Good news for all the people: For unto you [fourth-grade readers] is born this day in the city of David, a Savior ..." — a complete expression of God, a clear view of the eternity and cohesiveness of God's love, for all of us. This Jesus Christ is transcultural. It verifies all other "thin places" that have occurred throughout time: in a deed, a word, a confession, and a sacrifice, while also exposing any of our selfish human distortions of those revelations or our false claims to divinity.

But how can I convey that with words to nine year olds, that this Jesus Christ is universal good news?

I wrote, "Another Christmas story in the Bible tells of 'magi' or royal teachers from a distant country who traveled great distances to come to celebrate the birth of Jesus. Christians believe that Jesus Christ's message of God's love is for you and the whole world." My 350 words were almost all used up, but I had to write something about the end of the story! Human life has meaning and direction because God enters into it. Christmas proclaims that God comes totally into our living including our dying. Because of Jesus we know that God is among us and as close to us as one of us. The center and final future of all life knows us intimately and will not abandon us. The Easter end of the story that begins at Christmas claims that we need not be ultimately separated from unity with God and God's purposeful eternity.

In the northern climates of the northern hemisphere, I know that bringing evergreens into the home at the onset of winter as a symbol of life in the face of cold death and a hope for a life beyond death, that custom certainly pre-dates Christianity. But the Easter part of the biblical story ties this human hope to the nature and desire of God. But how do I say that in the closing of my brief article?

I wrote, "For Christians, Christmas celebrates God in Jesus coming into our everyday lives. And Christians believe that God will never abandon us but will be with us forever. This, too, is part of the story at Christmas. Many people bring an evergreen tree, representing God's everlasting love, into their home during the winter days of December. This 'Christmas tree' — this promise of life — often becomes the center of the family's Christmas celebration."

My article was completed. It was, of course, inadequate. I just hoped that maybe, by the grace of God, some school child might hear the invitation — might hear the Christmas angel say, "Fear not, for I bring you good news of a great joy for all people ... This shall be a sign for you; you will find a child wrapped in bands of cloth and lying in a manger."

Actually, we all have been given the same assignment that was given to me, to retell, from the heart, this Christmas story to our children and neighbors, and to ourselves, in words and ways that they can feel the love and know the grace of God. We all have been given this assignment. Perhaps through you they will hear the invitation, and perhaps accept the invitation. "And so, the shepherds said to one another, 'Let's go to Bethlehem and see for ourselves this thing that has happened, which God has told us' " (Luke 2:15 cf).

"This is the dawn of redeeming grace." Emmanuel — God is with us. Have a very merry Christmas. Amen.

Sermon delivered December 24, 1999
Weaver Chapel
Wittenberg University
Springfield, Ohio

Saint Stephen, Deacon And Martyr
2 Chronicles 24:17-22; Acts 6:8—7:2a, 51-60

Living And Dying

For we have heard him say that this Jesus of Nazareth
will destroy this place and will change the customs that
Moses handed on to us. And all who sat in the council
looked intently at him, and they saw that his face was
like the face of an angel. — Acts 6:14-15

Grace to you and peace from God our Father and the Lord Jesus Christ.

A few years ago, during the Christmas season in Philadelphia, a lonely and confused man, shoeless and shirtless, climbed to the top of one of the huge stone eagles that overlook the Schuylkill River. He stood at the top and looked down at the icy water below. Life to him no longer had real meaning or at least was one big disappointment.

As he contemplated the end, he cried out again and again, "Nobody loves me. Nobody loves me!"

His feelings seemed to have been confirmed when the usual crowd who gathers on these occasions answered his cries of distress and anguish by yelling, "Jump, jump."

Finally, after several hours, a priest with outstretched hands convinced the man to climb down from his perch and allow someone to help him. The crowd, disappointed in this conclusion to their wait, booed as the priest led the man down. To them this was a disappointing end to a long and cold wait. The poor, lonely man meant nothing to them except perhaps some possible excitement to liven up an otherwise routine, dull day. The fact that he was a person, a human, a life, had no significance to them; he was considered virtually nothing.

Something seems wrong about the theme for today. Our bulletin cover this morning has a nice, bright picture of the Mother and Child — Mary and the infant Jesus — the ultimate Christmas motif. Then on the inside, the little picture on the cover of the bulletin insert shows a person on his knees who is about to be clobbered by some big rocks held by two people on either side of the kneeling person. Something seems wrong today.

You come to church the day after Christmas and hear the assigned Old Testament lesson, which tells us a story about an obscure Old Testament character who is stoned to death on the steps of the temple by an angry mob of old friends. He is a character who manages in his last breath to call out for revenge against the king who allowed the stoning to occur and then, a few verses later, the king is assassinated in his bed. This is the season to be jolly!

The day after the symbolic giving of presents in supposed love and care, the day after the joy of the baby in the manger, we hear the epistle lesson retell the story of how Stephen was dragged to the outskirts of the city by another angry mob and also stoned to death. This is the "Joy To The World" season!

The gospel lesson for today is sort of a biblical summary of all the Old Testament instances of bloodshed from innocent Abel up through the stoning of the prophets. And if this isn't enough to dampen your Christmas joy, the sermon begins with the story of an attempted suicide.

Maybe the message of Christmas joy is present here for the Christian just as it is present in every situation at any time during the year. God's love, God's plan for life, came clearly for us into the human situation; it is symbolized in this time of year as a baby in a manager. We see in this event the coming of the Christ. The Christ is God's answer to those who stand on the peak of despair, contemplating the icy waters that seem to be everywhere, and just as importantly, Christ came for those who yell, "Jump!"

The Messiah came for all people, for us, for those who are dying, and for those who are throwing the stones today.

I was greeted by a news-film of all the Christmas Eve and Christmas morning fires in the greater New York area including close-ups of charred Christmas trees. The main story was a fire that killed an off-duty fireman and his wife. His fellow coworkers and friends who helped to put out the fire sadly told the news reporter what a nice guy their friend had been before his Christmas morning death.

The next item of news was about a mother who took her two young children to a department store on Christmas Eve. She had saved money to buy the children a toy for Christmas and since she wanted it to be a surprise, she had them wait for her in another nearby department of the store until after she made her purchase.

A few minutes later, when she came back to pick up her children, they were gone and, as of 11 p.m. of the next day, had not been found.

As I watched television Christmas evening, they had special on-the-spot coverage and a reporter, in his usual tactful manner, ask the young, frightened mother, "What is it like to lose your children on Christmas Eve?" Of course, the mother burst into tears.

If this wasn't enough to put a damper on Christmas joy, nothing could. For a moment, I was depressed, but I tried to work through this feeling. There is something more to Christmas. Christmas isn't an island and it doesn't really have distinct borders. It can never be over for another year. Christmas joy is one that intertwines and engulfs the realities of our existence, in our everyday world.

I read a good article in a journal about this reality of Christmas, this insight into the meaning of Christmas. The title of the article was, of all things, "The Death in Christmas." The author's insight into Christmas was gained when he received a card with a Christmas letter in which a friend spoke of having recently come to terms with the death of her father the Christmas before.

She wrote, "I think I've come to an understanding of Christmas that cannot be separated from death." There is a key here, for there is death in Christmas.

All the ancient biblical texts remind us of this. The baby in the manger grew up and was nailed to a cross as a sign of the death and the life of Christmas. The gospel of Matthew includes in its Christmas story, "Herod, when he saw that he had been tricked by the wise men, was in a furious rage, and he sent and killed all the male children in Bethlehem and in all that region who were two years old or under" (Matthew 2:16 RSV). Stories of suicides and stoning were in the original Christmas story, and the same presence of death is in every Christmas story since then.

We see it today in violent street crime and in a Pakistani mother watching helplessly while her infant child dies of starvation. We meet it in the blanket-wrapped remains of a woman dug from the rubble of a Belfast restaurant or in a cellar in Beirut or when a loved one dies of old age.

We can try to block it out, turn off the television set, turn up the Christmas music, turn away from the real conflicts of people, and watch another football bowl game. But death is still there even if we try to ignore it as our own loss, because it is inseparable from Christmas, for it is here that the real meaning of Christmas has its power.

The light of Christmas, that rich and ancient symbol, is always a light that shines in darkness. And when the darkness is not recognized, then the light is not seen. It is only against the surrounding gloom that the candle of Christmas burns bright. It is only over, against, and in full recognition of the reality of human suffering, inner turmoil and death that the new life of Christmas can be perceived and can be received.

Death as a part of Christmas is not only an external thing, death-out-there, the death of those poor children; it is also, and even more profoundly, an internal personal death that we face in the message of Christmas. Christmas is a measure of the passing of time, our time, our life. It is a milestone on the way to what?

It was the genius of Charles Dickens who saw that only when Scrooge was confronted, in that terrible vision of Christmas still-to-come, with this own grave, his own tombstone, that he discovers and, for the first time, accepts life — a life that for Scrooge is expressed in loving and giving and the totality of the spirit of Christmas. For us, too, for we are all Scrooges at heart; the death that surrounds us at Christmas, the death that confronts us at Christmas, shocks, appalls, and terrifies us. But if we are honest, if we are receptive, if we are open to the mystery, the grace, the gift of Christ at Christmas, it can also bring us to life.

In the beginning was the Word and the Word was with God, and the Word was God. The light shines in the darkness ... and the Word became flesh and dwelt among us, full of grace and truth.

— John 1:1, 5a, 14a (RSV)

For this is the message which you have heard from the beginning ... that we should love one another. We know that we have passed out of death into life, because we love our brothers and sisters. The person who does not love remains in death. — 1 John 3:11, 14 cf

Here is the message of Christmas, of the heart of God in the heart of a baby and in the heart of our darkness. The message is that death is defeated, and can only be defeated by the willingness to die in love; life is found in the very act of losing it, in the very moment of our readiness to give it away. The gift of Christmas bears the infinitely vulnerable, eternally powerful form of a flower, a flame, a flake of snow, and the flickering of life in the heartbeat of a newborn. It is delicate, but it is also beautiful and eternal.

Giving in the fullest sense of the spirit of Christmas is truly receiving — receiving life, receiving love, receiving joy in abundance, pressed down and brimming and running over and over and out through all of the eternal days of our living.

This coming week we will begin the Epiphany season and celebrate the light of God coming through Christ to all people. But before we enter that phase of the liturgical year, this rare second Sunday after Christmas gives us the opportunity to celebrate the light that shines into our own hearts through a faith relation with Christ, our Lord and Savior, the one who reflects the direction of existence.

The Word became flesh. God's Son was born in the days of Caesar Augustus in a barn to a Hebrew girl named Mary. Our whole earthly life has been invaded and changed by God in Jesus. This is the incarnation. This is Christmas — that it can be glorious to be human, as we open up to a Christ-filled humanness for ourselves.

Christ gives purpose and meaning, so there is no reason to jump into the icy waters of despair. Christ offers help and peace and forgiveness to those who yell "jump" at others in depression or pain and who selfishly throw stones or destructive words and thoughts at others.

Christ offers life in the face of death. So even on St. Stephen's, the Martyr Day, a day to remember a Christian's violent death, even today, and especially today, rejoice, "For to you is born this day in the city of David a Savior, who is Christ the Lord" (Luke 2:11 RSV).

The peace of God which passes all understanding keep our hearts and minds through Christ Jesus. Amen.

Sermon delivered December 26, 1976
Evangelical Lutheran Church of the Resurrection
Hamilton Square, New Jersey

The Epiphany Of Our Lord
Isaiah 60:1-6; Matthew 2:1-12

Light And Darkness

And the light pierced the darkness of it all, of it all — the Epiphany of our Lord.

> *Now when Jesus was born in Bethlehem of Judea in the days of Herod the king, behold, wise men from the East came to Jerusalem, saying, "Where is he who has been born king of the Jews? For we have seen his star in the East, and have come to worship him!"*
> — Matthew 2:1-2 RSV

I am very fond of the Christmas carol, actually an Epiphany carol, "We Three Kings Of Orient Are." I have always liked it because I can sing it rather comfortably, at least in comparison to most Christmas hymns. The carols about angels, for example, seem to be sung in such a high range that I become very self-conscious about my voice, not that it might be off-key, which I am afraid it is at any range, but rather, that it might be squeaky.

Christmas hymns about angels are sung high, I suspect, in some symbolic reference to highest heaven, above the mundane. Most were written in an age, which was much more comfortable with such special symbolism. But "We Three Kings" is more down to earth, sung in a lower range, more earthly, more grubby.

"We Three Kings" is easier for me to sing, but it also carries some profound insights into the meaning of Epiphany. Epiphany is an appearance of the holy, the most high God intersecting our personal, earthy existence. Just as importantly, Epiphany is God touching down and extending the gift, but it is also the finite human accepting the gift — the holy and human touch — maybe even an embrace.

"We Three Kings Of Orient Are" emphasizes those moments of divine grace and human acceptance and obedience. Remember that the gift in this Epiphany Bible story is not the gold, frankincense, and myrrh; the gift at the center of the story is the holy child. The acceptance was when the magi knew the meaning of the star and knelt in worship before the holy in the child. The gold, frankincense, and myrrh simply told about the child; the light of the star reflected through the child.

We three kings of Orient are;
Bearing gifts we traverse afar,
Field and fountain, moor and mountain,
Following yonder star.

They are human, but who are they, these magi?

Now don't be misled by the hymn. The magi according to scripture were not necessarily three, not kings, and not from the Orient. The small gathering of Christians who first read to one another the prototype of the gospel of Matthew envisioned an undisclosed number of searching magi bearing three gifts. Not kings, but magi who were perceived as rather mystical, magical characters from beyond the eastern horizon, Neo-Babylonian or Persian astrologers, searchers into the gods of the heavens. They were priest-sages, wealthy scholars, mystics, specialists in medicine, religions, astronomy, astrology, and magic. These were magi, Eastern intellectuals, coming not really from the Orient but from Iran or Iraq, from old Babylon, Persian pagans from over the eastern edge.

To be faithful to the text, it is best not to pretend to know too much about them and who they were and where they came from, except for the fact that they were mystical, magical, and yet fully human; in fact, they symbolized humanity's most precise attempt to find meaning in life. They were the epitome of human accomplishment, the high point of human knowledge and insight in the Near-Eastern world, the known world. They were the humans at the outer edge of the search.

According to the Matthean story, it was some magi who discovered the meaning of the God-light and in faith accepted its will and, therefore, bowed down before the point where that light intersected the human, full revelation in Jesus of Nazareth, an Epiphany of God, the divine self-disclosure — this event as transcendent and transcultural — universal. The magi now knew, and you can see it in their gifts.

> *Born a King on Bethlehem's plain,*
> *Gold I bring to crown him again,*
> *King forever, ceasing never*
> *Over us all to reign.*

This is true God piercing the center of history in the potential of a poor Bethlehem baby, potential fulfilled according to the end of Matthew's story. God was revealed through the action, personality, sexuality, and cultural, historical grounding of a brother — Jesus — this was the true God here enfleshed. The true God is that to which all genuine worship is addressed in any religion, to which all the burning frankincense, like candles and incense and smoke of worship, is hopefully addressed in all religions.

> *Frankincense to offer have I;*
> *Incense owns a Deity nigh;*
> *Prayer and praising, all men raising,*
> *Worship him, God on high.*

And all of the God-gift and promise is here in this Epiphany story.

Sidney Pitts was the organist of the church I served in New Jersey a number of years ago. Sidney invited me to his home for a vegetarian dinner one winter evening. He had bought a variety of exotic spices at a Princeton gourmet health-food store, even some spices the recipe didn't call for. Sidney liked to experiment in music and food. He bought and added myrrh to the wild rice, and just about poisoned us. Myrrh is an aromatic resinous powder once used in the preservation of dead bodies. You don't eat the stuff. What was it doing in a Princeton gourmet health-food store anyway?

Like Matthew's narrative, symbols of death along with genuine death pop up in all places. There is no escape, no excuse even for the rich magi in places like Princeton and Wittenberg, just like there was no escape from death, eventually, for the baby sleeping before the worshiping magi of Matthew's story.

> *Myrrh is mine: its bitter perfume*
> *Breathes a life of gathering gloom:*
> *Sorrowing, sighing, bleeding, dying,*
> *Sealed in the stone-cold tomb.*

The Matthean story of the magi actually holds a lot of myrrh.

> *Then Herod summoned the wise men secretly and as-*
> *certained from them what time the star appeared; and*
> *sent them to Bethlehem, saying, "Go and search dili-*
> *gently for the child, and when you have found him bring*
> *me word, that I too may come and worship him."*
> — Matthew 2:7-8 (RSV)

Just beyond our gospel reading for today are the screams of children and parents as the slaughter begins. Matthew didn't intend to stop the reading where we did this morning. The story continued with Herod's soldiers cutting the life out of male babies in Bethlehem. The story continues into the stacks of bodies the day after in Bhopal, India, and into the refugee camps on the Thi-Kampuchian border, and extended to the fresh cemeteries of Ethiopia. It continued in the image of the hollow-ringed eyes of urban poor; it continued into the walled compounds for political prisoners in the Soviet Union and South Africa.

"Bring me word, that I, too, may come and worship him." Worship him with a sword, with napalm, with a firing squad; vaporize him with a human nuclear explosion of starlight?

But the gift of myrrh took on new meaning with this particular child. It was an epiphany of God, the true God. All the forces of evil, of darkness, of chaos, of brutality and violence, even of death, and have no ultimate hold on the movement of God in this Epiphany, this manifestation, this revelation of God-ordained purpose.

God's future occurred, then and now, in the Christ for us. Myrrh took the form of a cross, but violence, suffering, injustice, and even death did not have the final word. The Epiphany of our Lord is today and it comes again and again for us. The epiphany of God is in bread and wine and world. Epiphany remains true through servanthood and mission in the midst of pressing human concerns of hunger, peace, justice, discrimination, and oppression. This action is taken, and faith is lived when we kneel with the magi before the true Christ, God for us, God offering the gifts of perfect light.

> *O star of wonder, star of night,*
> *Star with royal beauty bright,*
> *Westward leading, still proceeding,*
> *Guide us to thy perfect light.*

And the light pierced the darkness of it all.

> *Glorious now behold him arise,*
> *King and God and sacrifice;*
> *Alleluia, Alleluia!*
> *Sounds through the earth and skies.*

Amen.

Sermon delivered January 6, 1985
Weaver Chapel
Wittenberg University
Springfield, Ohio

Note: The hymn verses used throughout this sermon are from "We Three Kings Of Orient Are," words by John H. Hopkins, 1857, in the public domain.

The Baptism Of Our Lord
Isaiah 42:1-9; Matthew 3:13-17

Epiphany Hiking

*And when Jesus had been baptized, just as he came up
from the water, suddenly the heavens were opened.*
— Matthew 3:16

Reading again from our first assigned biblical text for this day,
this scripture from Isaiah 42:

*Thus says God, the Lord, who created the heavens and
stretched them out, who spread out the earth and what
comes from it, who gives breath to the people upon it
and spirit to those who walk on it: I am the Lord. I have
called you in righteousness, I have taken you by the
hand and kept you; I have given you as a covenant to
the people, a light to the nations, to open the eyes that
are blind, to bring out the prisoners from the dungeon,
from the prison those who are in darkness.*
— Isaiah 42:5-7

Woven throughout our holy scripture, and certainly dominat-
ing our assigned readings during the Epiphany season is the theme
of "light" versus "darkness." In describing the human condition
the metaphors of "light and darkness" are transcultural and are used
by all religions, including our contemporary secular religions; they
are the primary symbols in our poetry and film and advertising
today, used in all serious attempts, it seems, to probe the human
condition — light versus darkness.

I want to spend some sermon time probing this theme of "light
and darkness" today.

The word "Epiphany" comes directly into English from the Greek and means "appearance" or "manifestation" or "revelation." The literal sense of its verbal cognate is to "shine forth fully." It means to cast light upon something important so that we can see it clearly — sharply, perhaps for the first time. Experiencing an epiphany is to be "enlightened" — making manifest that which was previously hidden or unseen.

In the early church and retained later by the Orthodox church tradition, the Feast of the Epiphany of cur Lord on January 6 became the day to celebrate both the starlit birth of Jesus before whom the magi knelt — divine light penetrating the darkness, and pointing the way to Jesus, but also it is the festival day to read the scripture texts describing the baptism of Jesus. In fact, in the Orthodox tradition, our Lord's baptism was considered the most striking of the epiphany stories, for by God's grace it was here that the adult Jesus was revealed as the Christ, ready to begin a ministry for all people, offering light in the midst of any darkness anywhere.

It's hard to believe, but less than four weeks ago the snow and the temperature had not yet fallen. Mid-December was a rather mild beginning to the season. On December 14, I went for a long walk on the Superior Hiking Trail. I was very anxious to get out and hike knowing that those open trail conditions would not last much longer. My work schedule and the deer-hunting season had kept me out of the forest for a few weeks. Even wearing blaze-orange and trying to stay within state park lands was not safe during hunting season, I was told. So other hikers and I had to wait for the shooting to end. December 14 was the first opportunity I could get away, and it was miraculously, an incredibly beautiful, autumn-like day. The sun and the temperature were to rise from a nighttime 25 degrees or so, and soar up into the high 40s by midday.

My wife, Shirley, had to work that Monday, so I went to hike alone. My goal was to walk along the ridgeline from Tettegouche State Park to Bear Lake which is above Silver Bay, and then back again — about fifteen total miles. I intended to get an early start, but the roads were coated with a thick frost that morning and Route 61 was rather slippery above Two Harbors. I waited a while to let the rising sun burn the ice off the roads. It was within a few days of the winter solstice, and the sun slept in before leisurely arising from the lake, and never really arched very high in the sky. When I finally got up to Tettegouche, around 10:30, it was a bright and glorious early winter day; a sharp blue sky shown through the stark poles of white birch. There were no other cars in the parking lot, no other hikers, and I would not see anyone else the rest of the day.

I started the hike at a fast pace. It was a naked forest seemingly revealing all its secrets, no obscuring foliage or snow blanket. The trail was perfect — the potentially muddy sections were frozen and would remain frozen. It was all quiet; meeting a grouse along the trail startled both of us. The whole forest floor was covered with leaves, and occasionally the path was hard to follow, especially where it would cross a deer trail, or where the hiking path would join a snowmobile trail for a while in the shallow valleys and then veer off again. It was easy to miss the cut off, but I rarely ever get lost and usually know pretty much where I am on the trail. I was joyful at the prospects of the day ahead.

It was wonderful hiking. The bright, low sun cast long shadows of filtered light. I often stopped to take photos of the texture of bark on a tree, or the orange lichens on a rock. The water ran fast and foamy in the swollen creek beds. Because of the late start, I pushed myself and made it up on the cliffs above Bear Lake in time for a late lunch of a granola bar and water. Both Bear and Bean lakes were frozen over, and there was a cold wind coming off the valleys below, but in the sunlight on the rock cliff edge where I sat above the valley, it all seemed safe and comfortable and I could see, it seemed, almost forever.

Watching the clock, I started back. I knew the main trail fairly well, so I also took all the spur trails that offered views of Superior on one side of the ridge, and the forested valleys on the other. I checked out all the campsites and made mental notes on the best locations. In the meantime, the sun was, from our human perspective, descending. Actually, my location in this world was spinning away from the sunlight. I was moving away from the light, from a sun that never reached high in the sky that mid-December day and seemed to be in a hurry to exit. Where the trail would dip down the east side of the ridge spine, all would be in a total gray shadow.

The temperature was also dropping fast. I maintained the pace I thought was needed to emerge from the forest at my car by 4:15 or so. Half past four would be the latest to safely get out of the woods. Soon after that time it would be too dark to distinguish the leaf-littered path. I had brought in my backpack a flashlight, water, a Polartec jacket, gloves, and a hat. If I would have broken an ankle or torn a knee, I could have uncomfortably but safely spent the night in the forest. Shirley knew what trail I was hiking. This was not a life-threatening situation, but as the sun lowered in the sky and darkness seemed to creep through the trees, there was an emotional, even spiritual, alteration of mood and meaning.

The forest that had been so joyful and hopeful in the morning light was becoming a place of discomfort bordering on fear or dread. I began to lose confidence in staying on the right trail home. The later in the afternoon it became, the more aware I was of the importance of not making any mistakes, not losing footing on the ice-glazed rocks. But I am human and I make mistakes. As I became tired it was easier to trip over roots concealed by the leaves. I no longer saw beauty in the icicles hanging from the surrounding rocks; there was little light left for their crystal bodies to reflect. The quiet was no longer calming but rather a sign of abandonment. The naked trees became ominous. Coming across garbage left by the hunters weeks before — a plastic box that once held bullet shells and an empty pack of cigarettes — generated a sadness within me. As it became darker, the darkness became depressing. I wondered if this was all just a metaphor for life. One's life begins with great expectations, bright and cheerful, of facing the challenges of the new day — expansive plans and goals — climbing the mountain as a challenge. Then there are those moments of being hurt or deeply disappointed and those moments of hurting other people. The pilgrimage can seem like a journey into increasing darkness. Is this the end of our stories in darkness? Is this the progression of aging? Is death the final grip of the darkness?

To be alone as the shadows lengthened, one wonders if he were mistaken about the beauty of life. To be dependent on oneself alone and then to realize that cannot give us peace is so depressing. Depending only on one's cleverness, one's own wits and luck, is a life lived in the fear of becoming lost, or being left alone in the darkness, in a prison of darkness as Isaiah put it.

I received a Christmas gift this year from Shirley, a book titled *The Promise of Winter: Quickening the Spirit on Ordinary Days and in Fallow Seasons*, written by Martin Marty, a Lutheran church historian who teaches at the University of Chicago. The book also contained photographs of ice and snow taken by Marty's son, Micah.

Martin Marty wrote this in the book's forward.

Is the promise of winter spring? Not in this book. Here we use the image of winter to describe a condition of our hearts on ordinary days in every season. Here winter refers to the quiet times, the occasions when we lean back to search our interior lives. It represents some of the "down" sides that come every ordinary day — disappointments, setbacks, frustrations, puzzlements, and even temptations to doubt and depression and despair. To employ spring as the metaphor for whatever improves that condition would be to suggest that winter itself has no promise. Yet it does.[1]

Winter has its inevitable place in the human condition, but there is a promise offered even here, in the quiet times and for the interior life. The promise comes from what we [know] as the [creative] word of God. It represents here and now, for this day and [any dark winter] moment, a sense of the Presence [of God] realized each day, each night, with no waiting for spring.

Today, much spiritual writing makes it seem as if life can be all simple joy and ecstasy, [that in faith one will always] smile and be sunny, and instinctively and instantly come up with "praise-the-Lords." The biblical writers do not make such claims. They carry us into the depths and through them. [They] do not cheat and offer evasions or easy solutions. Realism colors all that they say, [yet] reasserting the promises of God in the midst of our winter. Strengthened by them, we find that our days, though they may not turn to spring ... [are not times of abandonment].

I emerged from the forest right at 4:15, and so can you.

In the country of Greece on Epiphany day, businesses and schools close, and the devout believers, and many undevoted seekers, flock to the churches in the early morning where a special worship service commemorates Christ's baptism. Worshipers enter the church in the early morning darkness. Candles are lit and soon the nave is washed in flickering light. The gospel story of the Baptism of Jesus is read. The people are reminded of their own baptism. The priest then prays over the water in the church's baptismal font and as a baptismal hymn is sung, the priest immerses a cross in the blessed water. The priest splashes the congregation with water from the cross as a blessing. The priest gives to each family present a vial of the holy water to take home to sprinkle and sanctify the rooms of their homes.

The people emerge from the church in sunlight to return home for a ceremony of blessing their own homes, and to have grand Epiphany meals of celebration — perhaps salted smelts, fish roe patties, marinated lamb brains, fresh mussels and octopus, braised eggplant, almond pears, and baklava, with tiny cups of Turkish coffee that they call Greek coffee, and I am sure some celebrative ouzo.

Then, in the bright sunlight of midday, the congregational members make their way down to the harbor where a crowd gathers. At a given signal, the priest throws the baptismal cross into the water to sanctify the sea. Young children dive in for the honor of retrieving the cross and returning it to the priest. But all the waters are now blessed as if they are in the baptismal font, and these waters flow out to surround the seaside and island towns. These waters join with all the global waters so that there is no place that is separated from the promise, from the offered, creative presence of the Word of God — light into any darkness. And, we have all been baptized with that water!

We began our worship this morning with a shared confession: "We confess to you God that we choose to walk in places far from your light. We neglect opportunities to do justice, to love kindness, and to walk humbly with you. We hide the light that is your gift to us. Forgive us and guide us on our way, that we may shine before others and give you the glory."

Pastor Ellenson responded with the offered word of God: "Arise, shine, your light has come. God forgives you all your sins through the wisdom and power of the cross, and has sent the Holy Spirit to rest upon you. People of God, live no longer in darkness, but in the light of Christ."

We will end our worship service this day with singing!

Lord, the light of your love is shining,
in the midst of the darkness, shining;
Jesus, light of the world, shine upon us,
set us free by the truth you now bring us.
Shine on me, shine on me:

Shine, Jesus, shine.
Fill this land with the Father's glory;
blaze, Spirit, blaze set our hearts on fire.
Flow, river, flow,
flood the nations with love and mercy;
send forth your Word, Lord,
and let there be light![2]

Amen.

Sermon delivered January 10, 1999
First Lutheran Church
Duluth, Minnesota

---

1. Martin and Micah Marty, *The Promise Of Winter: Quickening The Spirit On Ordinary Days And In The Fallow Seasons* (Grand Rapids, Michigan: William B. Eerdmans Publishing Company, 1997).

2. "Shine, Jesus, Shine;" words by Graham Kendrick, 1987. Taken from *With One Voice.*

Dream And Reality

How can one best understand Dr. King? What was it that formed and empowered him? To understand the primary influences in his life, one must begin on the western shores of Africa before the birth of this country, when the Portuguese first abducted a few blacks for slavery in Europe. To understand King, one must remember and feel the injustice and pain of millions of Africans forcibly transported from Africa to America.

At the age of six, King was told that he could no longer play with a white boy because he, King, was black. Shocked and hurt, King ran home. At the dinner table, his parents recounted the history of black people from Africa up to that particular Atlanta, Georgia, moment.

His mother then told him something that every African-American parent says to his/her children, "Don't let this thing impress you or depress you. You are as good as anyone else, and don't you ever forget it. You are an equal child of God."

King's maternal grandfather was A. D. Williams, who served as pastor of Ebenezer Baptist Church in Atlanta, Georgia. He told King's father that ministry properly understood involved not only the making of theological affirmations about God and who God is as defined by Jesus Christ, but that ministry also means the addressing of the gospel to the context and environment in which one finds oneself.

An Atlanta newspaper made racist comments in its editorial. From the pulpit, King's grandfather had some comments of his own to make. How can the gospel of love be changed to service? On one day, 6,000 Atlanta blacks decided not to buy that newspaper any longer, and the paper shut down. In 1931, Martin's father

91

became the new senior pastor of Ebenezer Baptist. He proclaimed the gospel and led a protest in Atlanta on behalf of the equalization of pay for black and white schoolteachers. It took eleven years, but he won the battle.

Martin King Jr. was ordained a pastor while still a student at Morehouse College. He decided to continue his studies at Crozer Theological Seminary and was graduated first in his class. He earned his Ph.D. at Boston University; his doctoral dissertation analyzed Paul Tillich's concept of God. For a young, popular, brilliant, black Ph.D. who could speak the language of European theology, there were some very nice teaching jobs in the Northeast universities and seminaries waiting for his decision.

He decided. He accepted a call to be pastor of Dexter Avenue Baptist Church in Montgomery, Alabama. He was grasped by the same forces that had held his grandfather and father by the Christian gospel of liberation for the oppressed.

He preached, and he also became the leader of the Montgomery Bus Boycott protesting the indignity of segregated seating. From the pulpit, King said at the very beginning of his ministry: "If we protest courageously and yet with dignity and Christian love, when the history books are written in the future, somebody will have to say, 'There lived a race of people, of black people, of people who had the moral courage to stand up for their rights. And thereby they injected a new meaning into the veins of history and civilization.' "

He won the bus battle, and the Civil Rights Act, and the Nobel Peace Prize, but the basic battle for liberation, for justice and freedom and peace, continued and continues.

Late in his career, King wrote the following.

Due to my involvement in the struggle for the freedom of my people, I have known very few quiet days in the last few years. I have been arrested five times and put in Alabama jails. My home has been bombed twice. A day seldom passes that my family and I are not the recipients of threats of death. I have been the victim of a near-fatal stabbing. So in a real sense I have been battered by storms of persecution. I must admit that at times

I have felt that I could no longer bear such a heavy burden, and have been tempted to retreat to a more quiet and serene life. But every time such a temptation appeared, something came to strengthen and sustain my determination. I have learned now that the Master's burden is light precisely when we take His yoke upon us.

There are some who still find the cross a stumbling block, and others who consider it foolishness, but I am more convinced than ever before that it is the power of God unto social and individual salvation. So, like the Apostle Paul, I can now humbly yet proudly say, "I wear on my body the marks of the Lord Jesus."[1]

If you don't have something worth dying for, you can't live free.[2]

On the night before his assassination, in a worship service in Memphis, King cried out his desire for liberation, which transcended race and creed.

What good is a desegregated lunch counter when you can't afford the meal? What do federal regulations desegregating housing mean when you can't afford a house? What does the right to work with people of all races mean when you can't find a job?[3]

On that last night, King preached the following.

Like anybody I would like to live a long life. Longevity has its place. But I'm not concerned about that now. I just want to do God's will. And He's allowed me to go up to the mountain. And I've looked over. And I've seen the Promised Land. I may not get there with you. But I want you to know tonight that we as a people will get to the Promised Land. So I'm happy tonight. I'm not worried about anything. I'm not fearing any man. Mine eyes have seen the glory of the coming of the Lord.[4]

I have a dream this afternoon that the brotherhood of man will become a reality. With this faith, we will be able to achieve this new day, when all of God's children — black men and white men, Jews and Gentiles, Protestants and Catholics — will be able to join hands and sing with the ... spiritual of old, "Free at last! Free at last! Thank God Almighty, we are free at last!"[5]

At five minutes after six on the next evening — April 4, 1968 — in Memphis, Tennessee, Martin Luther King Jr. was shot dead.

Let us pray: Gracious God we thank you for the gift, the courage, the example, and the faithfulness of your servant — Martin Luther King Jr. May we, too, be liberators, faithful to your word and will. Amen.

Go in peace, as messengers of justice and liberation, putting love into action.

Sermon delivered January 15, 1985
Weaver Chapel
Wittenberg University
Springfield, Ohio

---

1. Martin Luther King Jr., *Strength To Love* (Philadelphia: Fortress Press, 1981), pp. 153-154.

2. Martin Luther King Jr., *I Have A Dream, Writings And Speeches That Changed The World* (San Francisco: HarperSanFrancisco, 1992). Copyright 1986, 1992 by Coretta Scott King. Paraphrase of a speech given on June 23, 1963, in Detroit, Michigan.

3. http://www.religion-online.org.

4. Martin Luther King Jr., from a speech given on April 3, 1968, in Memphis Tennessee.

5. Martin Luther King Jr., from a speech given on June 23, 1963, in Detroit, Michigan.

About The Author

Born and raised at the Jersey Shore, Michael David Wuchter earned his undergraduate degree at Wittenberg University in Springfield, Ohio, then returned to the East for his Master of Divinity degree from the Lutheran Theological Seminary in Philadelphia, Pennsylvania, and his Doctorate of Ministry Degree from Princeton Theological Seminary. He became a third-generation Lutheran pastor. Wittenberg University honored him for meritorious service in 1983 and he was a Fulbright Scholar in India in the summer of 1984.

Michael Wuchter served The Evangelical Lutheran Church of the Resurrection in Hamilton Square, New Jersey, from 1972-1979. Wittenberg University, where both he and his wife, Shirley, had been students, called him to become the Pastor to the University in 1979. He served eighteen years as campus pastor before moving back to a parish setting in Duluth, Minnesota. Three years later, while on a mission trip to a companion congregation in Oniipi, Namibia, Africa, his life ended unexpectedly at age 54 on August 5, 2000.

Shirley resides in Duluth. The Wuchters' son, Andrew, and his wife, Traci, also live in Minnesota. The Wuchters' daughter, Kirsten, her husband, Bob, and their daughter, Elly, live in Montana.